Discovering The Other

Bernard Miller
Peter Johnson
Joyce D'Silva
Heiner Thiessen

ISBN: 9798364893833
© 2022 The four authors of this anthology
reserve the copyright to their
contributions individually

Kindle Direct Publishing

First Printing 2022. Printed in Great Britain by KDP
Cover Photo from www.canva.com
Cover Design & Layout: Heiner Thiessen
All proceeds resulting from the sale of this book
shall go to The Rosemary Foundation

Table of Contents
Introduction
Discovering the Other (5)

Joyce D'Silva

Heiner Thiessen

Introduction

Writing group members above from left to right:
Bernard Miller, Joyce D'Silva, Heiner Thiessen, Peter Johnson.

Discovering the Other

It seemed entirely improbable that we would ever come together as creative writers and to listen to each others' stories. But it still happened against all the odds and we became a real Writing Group some five years ago, never anticipating that we would last that long. Perhaps we realised that the actual writing and the subsequent discussions of our texts created a better understanding of each other.

5

Every new contribution shone a light on a personal landscape. What better way to discover the Other and to understand the formative forces of early life.

It has been a literary journey of discovery and of trying to disagree productively. It has also been a time of exploration about what we all have in common, despite the accident of birth and the influences of our early lives.

It took us a while to even become aware that we actually are an 'international' Writing Group with participants hailing from four different countries with their own political histories. And naturally we also discovered that each of us lives with his or her own thematic preferences, reassessing the past in autobiography or locating it again in fiction.

How did we ever get to the point of embarking on this journey of discovery? It seems that it all began with a brisk walk up Stoner Hill in East Hampshire. Coming away from the poet's stone, erected in memory of Edward Thomas, our local wordsmith, where Heiner Thiessen and Bernard Miller met, pausing long enough to reflect upon the silent wholeness of the landscape. Without the constraints of introductions, it seemed natural to exchange contact details.

There is an unwritten subtext to most meetings. A subliminal wisdom of accidents, perhaps? The past does not retire gracefully and squats in the shadows challenging the insistent claims of memory.

From the chance meeting on Stoner Hill, two became four. We began by writing about early childhood experiences. Gradually we discovered new layers of the personal past, digging deeper and focussing on topics that were close to our hearts. Personal experiences and current affairs came into it. We had all seen so much. It seemed fair game to reassess or reinterpret the past by shedding new light with the head torches of our advanced years.

So, here are some of our efforts, presented in four sections, one for each group member. Our thanks go to Bernard Miller, our mentor and one of the contributors, for his encouragement, confidence building and his stylistic suggestions.

Petersfield
December 2022

Bernard Miller

American born, I came to Britain in time for the Queen's Coronation with a theatrical production of my own. I've worked in London for years as a writer, editor and teacher in Adult Education, where I became aware of the largely dormant creativity in the ordinary lives of people. I've been intrigued by the way the British discard and reinvent their traditional loyalties and cultural commitments. I've also enjoyed the artistic diversity of other countries, working for an American newspaper in Paris during the 1968 student revolution, and finding a spiritual landscape among the olive groves of Deia in Majorca. I became a writer when I couldn't do anything else, being unhandy and easily distractible.

I am fairly rusticated now in Hampshire, where my companions in this volume often share the journey with me, confounding and questioning the years we've arrived at without our consent. It occurs to me that most knowledge, practical or esoteric, exists to resolve the elusive search for meaning. In fact, I am satisfied that the trip itself is the destination. Staying awake to the detours is always a challenge. I am grateful for the companionship.

Identity Crisis

My wife's mother had a stroke. My wife speaks of her as though she is no longer here, 'remember when mother did this or said that?' - meaning when she occupied space. When she was a person.

'She's still here.' I say.
'Her mind's not.'
'Her mind is busy elsewhere.'

My mother-in-law fell down a few months ago, turning her key in the front door lock, blacked out, scattering cut flowers about her as though to celebrate the fall, and awoke another person. That's what my wife thinks. She ransacks the lost luggage of her mind for thoughts that once housed words. I try sometimes to provide the words. Preferring her company to my wife's is no 'mother-in-law' joke.

'Her mind is gone.' Frances says.
'Her language doesn't work. She knows what she means. You expect her to mean something else.'
'She doesn't know me'
'Not the way you're used to. Maybe that's your problem.'

Stroke has added a new dimension to Freddie. An oddly compelling one. Reshuffled her priorities, trivialising crisis, ritualizing trivia. A restart of lost causes and the people who went with them. I could be one of them. Envelopes without contents recording her place in recorded time, the partner of a missing glove embracing a single gold earring and a wedding ring from one of her marriages. My wife is one of those oddments, dutifully tucked away, awaiting revision.

'My first born, your colouring certainly isn't mine. Or your hair. You're starting to look like your father.'
'Is that a compliment?
'I won't want to see him now. Tell him.'
'He's not alive, mother.'
'You needn't visit everyday, you know.
'Yes, I know that. This is my home. I live here.'
'You fuss too much. Let's have tea. I'm exhausted.'
'We've just had tea, mother.'
'Who are you, my Head Mistress? I can still boil a kettle.'

Frances is obedient, an obedient daughter. Letting go is difficult when your parent is your child.
'She'll burn the house down.'
'Leave her. She likes to cook.'
'I suppose you know she's incontinent.'
'I dribble a bit myself.'
'You don't need nappies yet. I can't spend all day with her.'
'Maybe she doesn't need you.'
'That's what you say about Em.'
Emma's our first born, doing her A Levels.
'Same difference. The old don't want much parenting, either.'
'I'm her daughter, for God's Sake!'
'That's what she can't piece together - what you expect of her.'
'I don't expect anything of her! I never have! I've never understood her.'

Frances wants comforting. I can't always manage it. An arm about her shoulders, maybe. Not much to ask. It seemed easier with her mother. Freddie was my friend. My partner in arms.

'Be a little sweet with her.' Freddie had once told me.
'Like you're not?'
'That's different. What does my neglect have to do with yours?'
'We're two peas, you and I.'
'For God's Sake, don't go believing that. I'm not married to the woman.'
'Do *you* love her?'
'What's love got to do with it? God, you're thick sometimes.'

I think I've stayed with Frances for Freddie's sake. My severest critic and unconditional friend. We are going to dry up and blow away together. That's what I told myself. If I split with Frances, I'll lose her mother.

'Why don't you let the Social Services help.' I asked Frances.
'Put her away?'
'Help her at home. Feed and bathe her a few times a week.'
'I can manage. For a while. I suppose we'll have to start looking around for a place.'
'I don't think so.'
'I haven't asked you. You're no help at all.'
I turn away, watch traffic. My attempted cool is a dead giveaway.

'Why don't *you* *t*ry looking after her!'

Not a bad idea, I'm semi-retired, but it wouldn't work. Freddie's outlived two husbands. I always felt she'd have been better off without either of them. They had the same Christian name and now she can't tell them apart. Jerry one and Jerry two. Freddie and I have always shared a special kinship. Like a shared secret. We seldom speak. I mean 'converse'. Polite conversation makes her sleepy. Before my marriage, she said 'You'll have to be patient. Frances feels she has to manage people.' A surprising indiscretion from a mother-in-law to be, but she was right. I learned to be a witness to a litany of still-born plans. If I kept silent, the grand schemes would usually vanish into a shopping list, or she would occasionally pause long enough to allow my opinion. 'Frances would rather you decided but she can't ask.'

"Your daughter has proposed marriage to me. Shall I accept?"

Freddie had introduced me to her daughter and taught me how to live with her. At first I thought she'd just off-loaded her unwanted baggage onto me. ("You never know someone until you share a bathroom with them", she said.) I was already middle aged and single in every way. I suppose it's like thirty-something women suddenly wanting to reproduce; if you don't try it you'll never know what it's like. Marriage is the same. The script goes: "Why have you never wanted to share your life with somebody." Shall I explain? Will you understand? My own company has always seemed like someone else. Like a whole crowd of someone else's. I've always envied people who know who they are when they're

14

alone. Freddie knows. "I'm one boring person all the time. My husband hated that. Men do. He didn't want the woman who made his bed to share it with him. I couldn't blame him. We agreed he would probably be happier with an affectionate housekeeper."

Freddie's healing presence often stilled the agitated enthusiasms of her daughter. More than once, Frances would retire early with nothing better than television to keep her awake, leaving her mother and me to walk the dog with scarcely a word between us. It was the time we both wanted.

'You're the only person who doesn't tire me' I told her.

We couldn't see each other in the shadows. She kept steering me off the flower beds.

'You tire *me*.'

'Well thanks!'

'I didn't say I didn't care. You drink too much.'

'No more than you.'

'Yes, but I do it for pleasure. Or for nothing. I don't hate my life.'

She knew I was smiling.

'I said Life, not Wife.'

We enjoyed preparing family meals together and escaping guests, and we played chess when Frances was in labour with our two sons.

'We can't really help' she said. 'Frances prefers labour on her own.'

'You mean she finds strength in suffering?'

'In sacrifice. I'm not much into the granny thing.'

'So I've noticed. What about motherhood?'

15

'I wasn't the worst. You don't want fussing when you're having a baby. You just want someone to pull it out. Stop the pain.'

'Frances doesn't think you've fussed enough.'

'Well, she plays to the gallery.' Her father applauded. I never could.'

She was right about that, and other things too. At 58, she was about to go back to University when Jerry, Frances' father, died - sell the family home and buy a one bedroom flat. Frances and Bertie, her brother, insisted that she needed family more than ever now, as a widowed person.

'I want a room with a kitchen and a bookshelf - that's all I need.'

'Frances will fight you.'

'I know. She won't miss a chance to interfere.'

'You might assume they're adults. Get on with your life.'

I offered my hand and she held on tight. We were at our most confidential scrambling up hillsides over rocks, keeping her dog away from the grazing animals.

'I'm sure you're right. Would we ever choose the families we end up with?'

Within months, Freddie had remarried. Someone she'd gone to school with. Jerry two had always made her laugh, she said, a stronger basis for marriage than groping around in the dark at their age. In fact, she'd lost her last chance of being a single person. Jerry two had a small timeshare villa in Crete and travel suddenly seemed as broadening as a university degree, so he sold his condominium and moved in with her until a joyriding adolescent knocked him down on a zebra crossing ten days after the nuptials. Freddie said, 'I haven't even seen him in his undershirt. We were going to consummate in Crete.'

At Jerry two's funeral we held hands. Freddie organised everything and as usual we colluded silently over the catering. While Frances welcomed and embraced the bereaved, her mother and I stuffed our faces with smoked sturgeon, caviar and champagne, the way the deceased would have wanted it. In fact it was all set up as if the late, not desperately lamented, were attending his own wake, wolfing his favourite charcuterie.

'I'd like to shed a few tears, you know?'she said, 'He was a nice man, he deserved a decent widow.'

'No man could hope for a better widow. I wish you were mine.'

'What's that supposed to mean?'

'I'd like you rifling through my effects, binning my image file by file.'

That made her cry, so I hugged her. A long hug. Frances passed with a platter of hors d'oeuvres. 'Come on you two – you can snog when the guests have gone.'

She recounted one of the daft entries from Jerry's emergency First Aid Pocket Jokebook for Flagging Festivities. It was about all he'd left her, that and rather a large number of bills and golf clubs. The Timeshare villa had gone to his daughter from a previous marriage. Frances found us again, laughing and choking on canape remains washed down with champagne.

'I didn't realise how much he meant to you, mother. Won't you want to join the bereaved?'
'Oh Lord, is my mascara running?'
I knocked back her champagne and mine and hiccuped.
'Good practice' she laughed, ' I shall be next.'
'Care to bet? You'll be pissed at my funeral.'
She was solemn now, guiding me by the hand to the remaining guests.

There weren't any more funerals for awhile. The least of her concerns. She'd booked herself on to a 'Singles Darwinian Discovery Cruise', from which occasional snapshots arrived: Freddie apparently engaging an Iguana in conversation, 'I'm the ugly one in shorts', and then Freddie on the waterfront, the arm of an athletically endowed young man draped casually about her shoulders. 'The only missing link I could find. We're studying finches together...' And then, solemn and alone, against the railing of the ship..... 'Home... none the wiser for Unnatural Selection... I'll ring of course.'

Which she failed to do. I did. Several times. Phoned and then dropped by, used her duplicate key and left a note... 'Still on holiday?' Still no reply. I phoned the airline, she'd arrived five days ago. Then there was a scribbled message by her phone, 'Don't be a pest, darling friend,...Drink my whisky....I'll call when I'm ready.'

She wasn't. And Frances booked her into a geriatric ward for stroke victims.

'We're moving her' I said.

'Oh yes? Private facilities? Day and night nursing?'

'We're taking your mother home.'

'So you can hold her hand?'

'She can hold mine. When you're busy.'

We seldom visited Freddie together. When we did, she turned her face away from one way conversations and slept, or pretended. Occasionally I would come alone and sit beside her bed without speaking. She would gaze at me for long moments, trying to find me a place. At times I thought I saw the trace of welcome. That's how I read her face. Actually I don't believe memory or its loss bothered her. She had left the future to fend for itself. Or so I imagined - having given her mine.

One day she held onto a small bunch of wild flowers I brought her.

'You married my daughter.'

'That I did.'

She selected a flower and gave it to me.

'Where shall we go?' she said.

A Graven Image

Robert Graves is sitting alone in my living room. In Deia, we leave our doors open to unexpected intimacy, and he let himself in. Just like that, there he was, obtrusively concealed in an alcove, giant poet and jealous lover, having probably searched the house for his current goddess figure, a white 'black goddess' named Cindy, one of his latter day literary evocations, far too matey for sex. With me anyway. There is a whole mythology about Graves' goddesses, black or white, which few understand, least of all the goddesses themselves. I try not to be startled by his celebrity, just in case I ever find myself included. "Cindy isn't here" I say. He seemed satisfied. Actually, he's rather sweet and convivial, with the edge of a stammer more affected than actual, to give him time to think, I think. And he's casual, or trying, like most important men in soiled Safari shorts, which is the gilt on the legend - a canny, conniving, physical performer in and out of verse. Or shorts.

The previous week, Peter Ustinov had peered through my window in search of nothing at all. Just happy to look about. On balance, I'm more comfortable with an uninvited raconteur than a celebrated poet. Ustinov refused tea and an offer to inspect my damp dwellings. Graves, like Ustinov, didn't trouble to introduce himself. I said, 'I've come here to write and I'm not writing.' He said 'You'll write when you need to.' 'Perhaps I need one of your muses', an indiscretion which died in the air and deserved to be buried. 'You are seeing Cindy?' 'Yes, everyday. Not intimately. You won't find her here.' He encourages frankness on his own terms. Writers traditionally settle in Deia to bask or grovel in his fallout. In the main, aspiring poets, 'tripping out' elusive epiphany on psychedelic drugs.

There was a time when Deia could consider itself the psychedelic capital of the Mediterranean. A psychic magnet in the Sixties. Many came to view its scenic wonders only to find themselves ditching their cameras to merge indefinitely with the landscape. They came, saw and snatched up available real-estate for 'spiritual and artistic regeneration' at increasingly premium prices. Graves has had only himself to praise or blame for its fame as a cultural commune. He saved the ancient village, its timeless aspect, extraordinary position and architectural integrity from the spoilers, the land developers destroying the coastal face of Spain. Faster than he would have liked, his presence, real or legendary, claimed the place for himself and his cast of minions, minor artists and itinerant seekers.

His permanent home ground in Mallorca, Deia has been Graves' personal squat since publication of 'Goodbye To All That', his celebrated autobiography of the thirties and beyond. He discovered the village after the war (he'd served in both) and never left. Like many expatriated Brits, he abjures middle class England, while affecting and manipulating many of its mannerisms. Standing in the shadows of my damp house, endeavouring to be fair, even English, he concedes I'm not dynamic enough to steal his muse, a minor disappointment. Cindy's role of Black Goddess to one of England's leading men of letters seems not ideal casting. She is not black except for her hair, but witty and gifted in her fashion (drawing and watercolour) and glad to be anything self-employed that's fun, even playing seasonal muse to Zeus of the olive terraces, however impermanent.

"Have you tried morning glory seeds? she enthuses, "Brilliant trip."

"They won't grow for me."

I had certainly given it a whirl. You don't live in Deia without tripping into or out of the self you came with. She hadn't read Graves before figuring in his writing.

"What do you think of his work?" I enquire.

"You don't write poetry to be understood, do you?" She asks without a trace of irony.

"Does he ever read to you in bed?"

"God no, I divorced my husband for that. He wanted me awake. Well I tried."

Graves is buried now in his beloved Deia, a conservation zone outside a chapel high above the village, as conspicuously anonymous as modesty will allow. One can just make out his name, a barely legible inscription scratched by somebody's grandchild, perhaps his, now flaking away in the wind. There is the occasional floral tribute. Not the one I hear when I'm alone with his remains. "Deia is the belly-button of the universe, but Fortnum's in Picadilly is still the best place for tea."

Miss Crawford Regrets
She's Unable to Sign Today

'Delivery for Miss Crawford.'

'Try the Trade Entrance! Do you need a guide dog?'

I'm not used to meeting movie stars on their home ground.
I'm trying to look official.

'I need her signature. Are you the maid?'

'Made in heaven, Junior. What is this? Give it here.'

Half of a familiar bone structure peered at me from under a
towelling turban.

'Sorry, I have to put it in her hand.'

'Don't be disgusting, Miss Crawford is indisposed until her
new contract arrives from her lawyer's office.

I didn't think movie stars answered their own doors. I didn't
believe they went to the toilet by themselves.
'I believe this is it.'

A hand shot out and made a grab for the envelope.
'I'm sorry, I can't. I have my instructions.'

'From where, little man - MunchkinLand?'

'I'm a Courier, Miss Crawford. From the Front Office. I have my instructions.'

The door swung open and there she stood, somewhat shorter than I imagined, barefoot and draped in Turkish towels.

'Who's instructing you?'

'Mr. Mayer. He says I'm to wait for a signed document.'

'L.B.? He knows me better than that! I don't sign without my lawyer, who happens to be in Palm Springs. Or you wouldn't be here. Right?'

'He says you've read it.'

'Several times.'

'He says you'll like it this time. He's added some figures.'

'What sort of figures?'

'I really don't know. Some zeros, I think.'

'It takes me a while to count zeros. I didn't go to Kindergarten.'

'There's no hurry. Miss Crawford. It's my lunch hour.'

This time she looked me up and down. I figured she slept in those eyelashes. The left one had come adrift.

'It will take me less time to read his obituary. Do you think he can wait while I bathe?'

She opened the door wider, inviting me in, turned and made her way upstairs.

'Ask the cook to give you some coffee!'

'I'm fine.' I called after her. 'I don't need coffee.'

'I do. Bring me a cup.'

By now she was at the upstairs landing, looking down at me.

'And some juice. Bring your 'reading material' with you. Take off your shoes.'

I found the kitchen. The cook handed me a prepared tray and laughed at my hesitation.

'Go on up. She doesn't mind company.'

She added a shot of clear liquid to the orange juice, vodka at a guess, and turned me in the direction of the stairs. I followed some vocal music to what turned out to be a bathroom. It sounded like Marlene Dietrich.

Crawford laughed at my expression. I hadn't expected to find her soaking in a bubble bath. She sang along with the verse: "Fallinck in love again, never vanted to, vot am I to do…cahn't help it…"

'Here, put that down.'

She accepted the tray from me, set it on a rack and knocked back the juice.

'Care to scrub my back and *sell* the story?' She laughed and tossed me a sponge. 'I'll deny it!'

She attempted another verse in fractured German.

'She's a great artist. I worship her. Here, give it some muscle. I'll bet all your women have dirty backs.'

In the distance, a doorbell chimed, followed by footsteps on the staircase. A man entered and took the brush from my hand.

'Who's Junior?'
'He arrived from Oz with a contract.'
'Want me to read it?'
'That's what you're paid for.'
'Not nearly enough.'
'Well, you have other bathroom privileges.'

She introduced the man as her lawyer, Greg Bautzer and dismissed me. My official look was fading.

'What shall I tell them?'

'She couldn't find a pen, or her reading specs' Bautzer suggested.

'Don't confuse the child, he's seriously intelligent. Working for Mayer big time, aren't you sweetheart? Going to own the studio one day?'

Bautzer pulled a document from his jacket pocket. I assumed it was a copy of the one I was delivering. Stars never signed up right away, which is why they had agents and lawyers.

'You're not going to do better than this, Joan.', said Bautzer.

'What makes you think so?'

'You've got the script approval you wanted.'

'Only I don't get the scripts. They go to Mother Superior.''

She was speaking of Norma Shearer, whom I happened to admire, the major MGM stock holder, veteran star and widow of the late Irving Thalberg, whose ingenious image making had turned Crawford from working girl of easy virtue to roles of elegant and tortured refinement.

'Hang in there, sweetheart.' said Bautzer, 'They're shooting her close-ups through lino.'

He glanced at the document in my hand and returned it.

'This is goodbye, Junior.'

'What shall I say.'

'How about "Inflationary pressures require reflection time." Or you could just say 'thanks, we're still reading the small print.'

I didn't wait to find out why Crawford's career at Metro was winding down. Movie stardom came and went with box office receipts.

'Will you tell her to bring up some more juice?' She called after me.

My shoes had gone walking. I found them outside as a limousine pulled up with L.B. Mayer's secretary. She had a briefcase full of documents and scripts.

'You can go.' She stalked past me.
'She wouldn't sign.'
'She'll sign.'
Her look was execution and burial in one go.
'What about this? I held out the failed delivery.

'Don't you know how to use the shredder?'

In fact it was Crawford's last MGM contract. Her overtures to rival studios for more mature roles, none lacking her sexual sovereignty, even won her an Oscar, and the enduring admiration of the public. I've always wondered what might have happened if her lawyer hadn't arrived. I can't think I was ever adventurous enough to find out.

Hollywood Children

The thing about being a Hollywood child is that there's no place to go but down. Adults can hit the skids and stage a comeback but a child can't be a child twice. We put our growth- hormones on hold and tried to reclaim them when we were through in pictures. By then it was too late. By the time we'd kicked barbiturates, speed and coke and escaped our ambitious mothers, we were middle aged. Nobody can make it back when the thrill of being discovered is gone.

It is axiomatic that great little personalities are simply not interesting in mature bodies. Shirley Temple was a terrible grown-up actress. She couldn't help it. She kept doing the thing that made her famous in the first place. Same baby voice, same adorable dimples. It seems somehow obscene to think of her cohabiting in later life. Margaret O'Brien? Gone. (Who would dare condemn the hoyden baby of Meet Me in St. Louis to a lifetime of maturity?) Jane Withers? Gone. Bobby Breen? Boy sopranos never fade away, they simply die with mature vocal cords. Freddie Bartholomew? Jackie Coogan? Unrecognisable. Jackie Cooper? Directs, even acts sporadically, recalling sex with Joan Crawford at 16, his ripest performance. (She bathed and powdered him first.) Whatever happened to Bonita Granville? A striking villainess of 12 (in 'These Three'), unremarkable as a junior sophisticate. The necrological inventory reads like a war memorial. We can protect our children from every pitfall but professional burial.

There were survivors, noted more for their sex appeal than talent. Elizabeth Taylor, Natalie Wood were employable. Even bankable in the case of Taylor whose private life prolonged her box office appeal and fed the gossip columns. Some were able to hang on as character actors, never having 'made it big' in the first place. The independent film companies were less crippling to their featured child players, rarely under term contract. It took the major studio system, the venomous sentimental paternalism of L.B. Mayer, to shorten the life of Judy Garland, with amphetamines to get her to work and sedatives to help her sleep them off.

Child performers of recent days are taught not to act which means with luck they might survive long enough to learn how. When I grew up, acting meant being precocious, showing off. Being natural meant *not* acting, sometimes called 'star quality'. The same child actors today would be expected to wander in front of the camera, only occasionally recalling why they were hired.

So why was learning your trade as a child the kiss of death? The inadmissible secret is that *one* life is really quite enough, and growing up can be more exhausting than growing old. To this day I've not understood how success works, not merely getting it, but *keeping* it. Do you work for it or wait for it? Do you believe in your employable self or carry ambition around like an inoperable tumour? A discrete retirement into autobiography, the reliable fiction of life, is surely the only solution.

Celebrated Progeny

The Chaplins are the two saddest boys I know. One is gloomy sad, that's Charlie Junior, although he does a fair imitation of his father's famous walk, twirling a cane and twitching his moustache. The other is sort of comically sad, that's Sidney, who probably feels he isn't really clever enough and struggles against odds to make you laugh. Charlie Junior wants to be left alone to get on with his sadness. He has the look of someone who expects nothing. I like him better than Sidney but he doesn't much like me, so I talk to Sidney who doesn't much care who he talks to. We're sharing a cabin at Camp Black Fox Military Academy, where all the movie celebrities dump their kids over the summer, and I guess I'm the only one without pubic hair which is embarrassing, so I undress under the covers. In the next bunk is Bobby Breen, boy soprano who's my age, eleven pretending to be nine so that his producer, Sol Lesser, can get three more soundtracks in the can before his voice breaks. Bobby has a lot of pubic hair for a child soprano and he climbs on top of me singing Victor Herbert ballads like Nelson Eddy to Jeanette MacDonald, "Ah Sweet Mystery of Life At Last I've Found Thee, Ah, at last I know the secret of it all…"

In the shower he says: 'Tuck it between your legs.'
'It won't go…'
'I'm not making love to a soprano with a dick.'
He crushes me against the wall.
'It won't work', I say lamely, 'I'm a baritone!'
'Never mind, I'm on fire!'

He takes aim and pees at me.

'This is so you don't get pregnant!

I have to be sweet to Bobby. His sister, Sally, gets Mama work in Bobby's films, and I have a speaking part in his next film, "Rainbow on the River". I play the snotty rich kid. "Make a Wish" is the last film we do together. We're in a summer camp, Camp Birchlake, just like this one, only now he's the big star so he doesn't mess me about in the showers. Anyway, kids are not supposed to know about sex. Their parents only do it to make babies. Unless they don't want any more kids and get divorced instead, like my parents did.

I hate summer camp as much as Charlie Junior.

'Who said I hate it?' he says.

He's by himself on the far side of the lake where people go to get away from people. It has a broken down pier with a sawed off plank for a diving board.

'I guess I thought you did...'

He's reading a comic which he makes a point of not putting down.

'I guess you don't want company.' I say.

'That's right.' He throws me a comic. 'I don't hate people because they're dumb. Most people are dumb. You're pretty dumb when you suck up to people with that phoney English accent. Makes me want to puke but I don't hate you.'

'Gee thanks. I only speak that way in plays.'

'Well, it sounds affected. You asked me, so I'm telling you.'

'I didn't ask you. Your father is English.'

'Not like you, thank God. What's there to hate about this place?'

'The other kids, I guess…mostly. You don't?'

'Kids are shit. You don't have to like them. You look scared all the time because they beat you at games. You ought to stop looking scared.

'I'm not.' I try to protest.

'Well, you look it. So terribly nice all the time. So veddy polite.'

I think 'you're as big a shit as everyone else,' and I start to go, and then I change my mind. I keep thinking how important his father is.

'What are you planning to do?' I ask him.
'Do when?'
'Are you going to act like your father?'
'Two Charlie Chaplins? Oh sure.'
'I think you imitate him very well.'
'I can do that in my sleep. What does your father do?'
'He's in business. It's really boring. I'm going to act, I suppose.'
'Are you any good?' He goes back to his comic.
'I think so.'
'Does anybody else?'

I heard Lew Ayres say 'I don't act for other people.' So that's
what I say. He smiles like he doesn't believe me. Like he'd
heard it before.
'I've been in a few films. I guess you haven't seen me.'
'I guess I haven't. I might have blinked. Bit parts?'
'There are no bit parts. There are only...'
'Lousy two bit actors – yeah, I know.'
'Are you in your father's movies?'
'Have you ever seen me in my father's movies?'
'I haven't seen them all.'
'How come?' I guess he wants to make me squirm.
'I've seen everything he's made since The Gold Rush.'
'Then you haven't really seen Chaplin. Let's go for a swim.'
'I think The Gold Rush is the best. And City Lights. The late
ones - like Modern Times. That was brilliant.'
He pulls off his jeans to swim bare ass.
'The ripest fruit is ready to die." says Charlie Junior,
'coming?'
'I don't think so...'
'Be a devil! I won't look at your genitalia! Unless you
insist!'
He manages a pretty fair dive. My grandmother told me if
you don't push doors they won't open by themselves. I take a
deep breath and push.

'I'd like to meet your father.' I shout.
'When?'
'Whenever.'

He disappears underwater for at least a minute. 'So would everybody, including the Chinese!' he gasps, 'So would I! Can you dive?'

'I'm learning. I've got an improvement medal.'

'Improvement?' He laughs. 'That's what they give to spastics! Here!' (*)

He climbs onto the diving board

'You can imitate me!'

He suddenly becomes his father, twirling an imaginary cane, tripping himself and falling in backwards. Halfway across the lake, he waves at me. I'm over my head and swallowing half the lake, but I wave back. I guess I learned too early – it was easier to imitate life than to live it.

We went our separate ways after that. He would catch my eye and grin as if he knew me, without speaking.

I suppose he learned to mime feelings from his father. He packed his things and left before the camp season ended, without saying goodbye.

....

Charles Spencer Chaplin Jr. had the look of someone without a future. I don't know what that means when you're eleven years old. As a rule, the children of Hollywood celebrities rarely manage an image of their own. Most of them retire before their parents. That is, if they live long enough. In fact, hardly any newsprint acknowledged his death at the age of 43, allegedly from an overdose. Celebs rarely breed celebs. Fast readers would be lucky to find him in his father's autobiography. The legendary comedian didn't admit failure, and by that time he was busy producing eight new offspring with the last of his child brides, the daughter of the celebrated playwright Eugene O'Neill, who despised his elderly son in law. It is generally understood that men of great fame and unusual sexual endowment prefer the children of their old age, with each arrival the challenge of renewed immortality.

A political exile from the United States, Chaplin's reproductive achievements tended to displace the critical failure of later years. His unique genius as a mime artist faded with talking pictures. And with it, his dream of reforming the unequal society that had brought him wealth and fame. In fact, the performing artistry of his lovable balletic tramp was the generous gift of laughter, hope, and forgiveness that the world needed during a century devastated by global warfare. It is sad that his sons were unable to enjoy the benefits of that extraordinary gift.

(*) The dialogue in this essay reflects US youth culture of the 1930s and is no longer acceptable.

'Cloning Orson'

'Who's that kid in Ruth's chair?' Ruth Warwick, for your information, the patrician and probably frigid first wife of Charles Foster Kane, known to cinematic posterity as 'Citizen Kane'.

Welles approached. 'This is a closed set.' He hoisted me to my feet.

'I'm here to watch you work.'

Orson thought I might be a friend of the producer. Producers don't like Orson. His movie is a kind of closely guarded open secret. The secret is that nobody knows what he's doing, while everybody does. He's on borrowed time till they find out how much his genius is costing them. For the moment it tops the budget of any film made by RKO, subjects of his own choice, and without interference from the front office. Nobody's had a deal like that before or since. He denies that he's filming a profile of the notorious newspaper publisher, William Randolph Hearst.

'I'm with the press. We want to talk about Kane.'

'Which newspaper?'
'The Hollywood High School Gazette.'

'I'm not ready to talk to the '*Hollywood High School Gazette*'! Blimey, whatever next!' he bellowed, with that resonant vocal instrument that stunted his growth as an actor. 'Don't kid me – you're a company spy!'

By now I was almost out the door. A security guard had seized my arm.

'Please let me watch. I'll stay out of the way.'

He squinted at me through Klieg lights. Welles at twenty-five looked sixty. He was wearing a bald wig.

'I don't know you, do I?'
'You will. I'm a walking oxymoron – like you.'
'Christ, where did you pick *that* up?'
'How did you learn to make a movie? You're a theatre person.'
'By making a movie. Sorry kid, no time to talk.'

At least he was decent enough to be sorry.

'Can I be your clapper boy?'

'We've got a clapper boy. How did you get through security?'
'I joined a tour – elderly trogs with autograph books. *Please* Orson, (I risked the overly familiar) I've come to learn from you.'
'Can't teach. Don't know how.'
'You won't know I'm here. I promise.

39

I understand how everything works.'

By now, the guard had me by the collar and was giving me the bums rush.

'How *does* everything work? You've got five seconds.' He checked his watch.
'If you won't tell me your secrets – I won't tell you mine.'

Welles winked at the guard and gave me something between a hug and a shove back onto the set. It was Susan Kane's bedroom.

'What makes you think you're me?'
'I've known what I know since birth. Until they try to teach me, and then I can't do *anything*. Every year of school I know less and less.'

'Here, finish my coffee.' He strode back into the lights. 'OK Commie,' he bellowed – 'let's break up the set.'

That's Dorothy Comingore, scarcely heard of again since Citizen Kane. They were doing the scene where she walks out on Kane forever and he destroys her bedroom with all of her priceless, tasteless objets d'art. Comingore peered in my direction and shared the joke with Orson, who called out to somebody. I think it was the Assistant Director or Greg Toland, the cameraman, somebody like that.

'Let's do our worst. My replacement is standing by!'

I'd made it! We're practically on a buddy basis. But then he shared a lot of other jokes where I *wasn't* included and went to the canteen without me. So I hid in the shadows until they started shooting again. It was a wondrous sight – all that wreckage to Susan Kane's room. Orson sat recovering and breathing hard.

'Can I get you something?
'Nope.'
'Like coffee or something?'
'Are you still here?'

'You were powerful – dynamic! Three takes! Where do you get the energy?'

He shook his head. He wasn't listening and I thought maybe I'd better back off. Instead, I pushed my luck.

'How do I get back in here tomorrow?
'You don't.'

I squatted on a crate.

'Look! I'll just sit and watch. Unless you need me for anything. You can just shout.'
'Hey John, what do I do with this kid? He's got gall and he thinks he's me.' He was trying to dislodge the bald wig.

41

John Houseman eyed me like something at the bottom of a fish tank.

'Let him watch – if he keeps out of the way.'
'We don't even let the producers do that.'
'Can you handle a broom?' Houseman addressed me.
'If you can handle the 'Sweepers Union', John.'

Orson grinned and disappeared to his dressing room, so I followed Houseman off the set trying to make intelligent remarks. He's a smooth number, cool and cultured. Upper class Brit, I thought.

'There's never been a movie like this.'
'You an Art House buff?'
'I'm a writer. I'm writing a film now.'

Houseman didn't seem impressed.

'Starting early?'
'Isn't *he*?'
'*He* is something of an exception.'
'Doesn't that prove the rule? I don't expect to live long.'
'Why is that?'
'I guess I've seen enough. Until maybe today. Most films are crap.'

He surveyed me from Olympian heights.

'Are you exceptional?'

I was modesty itself: 'If given the chance.'

'What are you writing now?'
'It's called '*Passport to Perdition*'.   It's about a community of dead people stuck in purgatory, only they don't know it and they're trying to discover *who* they are so they can get out. Maybe change their lives around. I look into each life.'
'That's fairly ambitious.'
'Yes. It's hard not to write too much. Every day it looks different from the night before. So it's getting longer than 'Gone With the Wind. And you can't get more boring than that, can you? I thought maybe watching him film his own script would make a difference.'
'Why don't you try something easier for your first script?'
'It's not my first. I've been writing since I was eight. It is all I can do.'
'How old did you say you were?'
'I'll be seventeen.'
'When?'
'In two years.'

He had reached his car. He was laughing. I guess I seem funny and it doesn't matter. It is the only way to influence people.

'How long have you worked for Mr. Welles?'

'*With* Mr.Welles,' said Houseman. 'Which way are you going?'

'I'm not sure.'

I was, but I'd run out of things to say. I had to get back on the set.

'I won't go out of my way. I'm driving to Brentwood, with a stop on the way.'

'Sounds OK. I'll go that way.'

He unlocked the passenger door for me. 'Where do you live?'

'I *exist* in Hollywood. Dead dump. A street with bars and souvenir shops. It used to *mean* 'Hollywood' in the old days. I'll take a bus home.'

He was silent for a while until we stopped for a signal.

'You think Orson can help you?'

'No one else can'

'Are you an actor too?'

'All the time,' I laughed. 'I've won awards.'

'Oh yes?'

'First prize in Dramatic Declamation for this state: '*Death Takes a Holiday*'. Want to hear my hysterical laugh?'

'Not if you can help it. What about films?'

'Have you got a part for me?'

'We're doing a season of theatre. In Santa Barbara. Maybe you've heard about it? Selznick's bid for culture on the West Coast.'
'You're working with David Selznick?'
'*For* David Selznick,' he laughed. 'You might come along. You won't get paid. You can assist the Assistant Stage Manager. Keep track of props, maybe learn the switchboard, without causing a Union crisis and general walkout. Care for a drink?'

We'd reached his stop. I must have looked surprised.

'Ginger ale or coke. Strictly kosher. After all, you're a minor. I don't want to get booked.'

His hand was squeezing the patella of my left knee. It was a relatively impersonal squeeze and I pretended not to notice. He reached across me and opened the passenger door.

'Go on – You won't be alone. I'm interviewing actors for Selznick.'
'I'd rather sweep for Orson.'
'Can't help you there. Try Santa Barbara.'

I did. I was the company mascot. I didn't have to do anything but be a terribly congenial juvenile, run for coffee and lunches, move props and collect 'the key' to the curtain (a company leg-pull at my expense) and avoid the company paedophile, which took a degree of tact. I told him my mother had booked the hotel room next to his and she was a light sleeper.

45

'I'm very quiet,' he said.
'I'm not,' I said.

I thought it best not to embarrass predators whom you may need on the thorny path to film fame. You'll never know when you're going to need them.

Citizen Kane failed at the box office, while becoming the most enduringly celebrated film ever to emerge from Hollywood. How, after all, can you do things better than anyone else at 25 and hope to survive a philistine society of corporate film giants? That's why I so desperately needed Orson. To follow wherever his footsteps led.

I turned up again, uninvited, on the set of 'The Magnificent Ambersons'. Only this time
I'd written him a letter, which he hadn't bothered to answer. I didn't expect him to.

'You certainly are an *original* pest.'
'You won't know how good I am until you let me work with you.'
'If you're so good you won't need me.'
'You know how to get money for art. What I mean is people *believe* you.'
'Maybe you're not a good enough liar.'
'*You* believe me.'

He laughed. 'You mean this is all bullshit about your genius?'

'Will you look at my script?'

'Could you tolerate the truth?'

'OK. Sure, why not?'

'I don't have time for you. Your need shows too badly.'

That hurt. He knew it.

'I'm sorry sonny. You're not a child or a man. If you're not careful, you'll fall through the crack.'

And he walked off. He wasn't an actor on that film. Merely a voice-over; a shade of the caricature that was soon to overtake his genius: 'I am Orson Welles – The Word made flesh, until Genesis is rewritten.' Genius seldom strikes twice in the same place. And there was no one to *clone* but himself.

At least he was true to his word. I sent him my script. My complimentary ticket to his legend, which the studio system did its best to destroy. He didn't read it.

An Amicable Divorce

He: May we speak candidly?

She: If you can be brief. I'm doing the double crossword. There's a nut roast in the oven.

He: I wonder - as we get older - if we are losing our faculties, or learning how not to care.

She: I'd guess in your case, it's a bit of both.

He: I don't mean about each other. I mean about life. You find me dull? Tell me – I can take it. Everything seems so utterly worthless. Whether I want something or don't want something. It's all the same thing.

She: Not entirely. Have I told you today that I want a divorce?

He: No.

She: I want a divorce.

He: Actually, you told me yesterday. And last Friday night at the Proms. I didn't believe you then, either. Just another piece of paper. Like a marriage licence.

She: Yes, but it's something permanent to hold onto. Something to cherish on long winter evenings.

He: I don't mind giving you a divorce if it makes you happy.

She: It would. Please believe me. I know it would and it would be something we haven't done yet.

He: We haven't been to India.

She: I'm not keen on India. The teeming masses. And the flies.

He: Not in the Rishi Valley. It's like Somerset.

She: There are flies everywhere in India. On your fork when you eat.

He: Well, how about the fjords. There are no flies in Scandinavia.

She: Too Wagnerian. I prefer flies to Wagner.

He: We've never done Kenya.

She: Flies! Flies! Flies! I want my divorce first.

He: We could try the Nile again? Under mosquito netting? You've always liked ruins. We made love at Abu Simbel.

She: I must have been drunk.

He: What sort of divorce would make you happy.

She: The permanent sort.

He: I see. (PAUSE)

She: Did that hurt?

He: Can we go on living together?

She: I don't see why not.

He: Because I would insist on that. You can keep the hamster and the tropical fish, but we have to go on sharing costs and sleeping together.

She: Twin beds?

He: Zip and Link. I have to know where you are.

She: On the other side of the zip? I'll need to talk it over with Rupert.

He: How can your divorce lawyer help us with our mattress?

She: His ex wife is my gynaecologist. She recommends zip and link prior to the final decree.

He: I'm losing heart.

She: Don't. After a year or two we can consider reconciliation.

He: Come here. Let me hold you.

She: (SHE COMPLIES) This is a pointless exercise.

He: But don't you see - we need each other or we wouldn't be separating.

She: I've never understood that.

He: Look at it! People separate to find out why they married in the first place.

She: I will always know why I married you.

He: I'm waiting.

She: I was ovulating heavily that summer.

He: You said I reminded you of Tony Curtis.

She: Boris Karloff. I've always fancied ugly men. My father was an ugly man.

He: You could hardly wait to get me into bed.

She: A Comedy of Errors. You were building muscle on steroids.

He: I forgave you your breast implants.

She: Women don't want forgiveness.

He: What do "women want"?

She: Indiscriminate lust. All the way to the cemetery. Forgiveness after the last rites.

He: I never thought the lust bit mattered that much.

She: It didn't – until it was too late. Everything good is always too late.

He: I think perhaps you've been watching me too much.

She: What makes you think that?

He: You've never had your own interests. You think married love is a way of life, whereas I've always thought of it as a habit I can't break.

She: You didn't mind starting up a new addiction with your secretary.

He: Are you speaking of that Sales Convention weekend? We were both too drunk to attend the meetings..

She: What a waste. Didn't she bring your Viagra from the office?

He: Jealousy is not your best suit. We both need outside interests.

She: I got an Honours degree last year while you were watching University Challenge.

He: I read Wikipedia faithfully!

She: Media tuition is for 'retards'. We need the company of other failed mystics.

He: Or nutritionists perhaps? I'm smelling burning cashews.

She: I've set the alarm!

He: Good thinking! Will you be needing the divorce after supper?

She: Have I ever denied you anything? We can finish the double crossword together.

I'll See You Again

So here I am again, finding her in another lifetime. She knew me of course at once, the moment we met exchanging platitudes on the bus. Neither one of us was even remotely interested in the weather. She knew I was waiting to get off at her stop. The most natural thing in the world, you might say, except for the 30 years or more that separate us from a conventional courtship. She wouldn't let me go, and we continued making small talk all the way to her door, and then, when I couldn't leave, she plucked a flower from a hedge and pressed it into my hand. Naturally, I knew what that meant. I can't invite you in. She had done the same thing in Ravenna in 1848, only then I was over eighty, and she was a music student barely out of her teens. It was always the same. Stay with me, there must be a way for us. And now, here, in this featureless semi detached road in Hendon, of all the dismal places to reencounter a reborn soul mate, we were once again holding each other at arm's length until one or the other of us should die.

In the meantime, she would keep me around for her pleasure, and marry me off to her daughter. I can hardly forgive her for that. I'm not going to pretend to be a good husband or a good father, but I do know that everything that is decent in my character comes alive when I am with Emile, with an E, as she is in this, her French incarnation. If she insists upon being my mother in law, how can I refuse? I know only that we are one person, and although she dare not admit it, we must ultimately be lovers to be truly ourselves. I cannot bear it – all these largely unnecessary lives trying to be one, in the right place at the right time - so we needn't be reborn. You see, we are two halves of the same life. How does this happen, and why am I telling you? You can't help. No one can. I don't believe in Providence or karma....we've laughed our way through that on many occasions. Our connection is no divine mystery. At least not to us. She did say, on one occasion, "what if I'm reborn a male person. Will it bother you?" "I suppose not if I'm a woman person" I replied. "And if you're not? Shall we be a same sex couple?" "As long as it's not transgender! I despise half hearted commitments. Let's play that challenging card when it's dealt us."

I'm too old for you now, I heard her thinking. What she said was "I'm looking after an invalided husband. Would you like to meet him?" "I don't know that I should. I might like him." "Why not?" she smiled, "I like him." And then we both had to face the agonising reality of not necessarily preferring each other to the partners rebirth had given us. We seemed to understand that we could no more change our destiny than the random one natural selection had granted the chimpanzee or mountain goat.

I found her once on the beach. She was five and a bit, and she let me save her from drowning. A sadly wasted opportunity to perish and revive together. She sat on my lap while I dried her off, and we sang together one or two nursery rhymes until her terrified mother appeared. She clung to me for a few moments before being carried away. It was pointless explaining that I'd known her child for a very long time. Several millennia, in fact. Longer than this mother, as a Virgin, had wept at the foot of the cross. I think we both knew it was our last chance to find each other lifetime.

Peter Johnson

Born in London but grew up in Surrey. As an unenthusiastic student, he scraped into the bottom of the top sets at school and was relieved to get away. Studying accountancy took ages but the eventual qualification led to an office-based life in various venues. He spent ten years in Greece to where he returns as often as possible. With a wife, two daughters and two grandchildren, he regards himself as content with life.

After the Shredding

It all started two years ago. A picture by a well-known artist that was up for sale at a leading auction house in London, suddenly started to shred itself as the auctioneer's hammer concluded the sale. The staff hurriedly removed the picture as this was not good for business but, too late, a video of the whole episode was soon winging its way round the internet. But this was just the beginning. A few days later, the BBC's morning bulletin was interrupted by an item of breaking news. Security staff at the Louvre in Paris had just discovered that overnight Leonardo's Mona Lisa had been crying real tears leaving a puddle on the floor beneath the frame. Subsequent analysis revealed that the liquid was indeed that of real tears. There was a public outcry for Inspector Clouzot to take on the case but his boss at the Surete insisted that he could not be released for another assignment until he had dealt with a mountain of paperwork. A reporter caught him in the street and asked what he thought was at the bottom of the mystery. All Clouzot could answer was that it needed thorough investigation but he would not be surprised if the Russians were behind it. This idea did not hold water for long as later that evening news came through from Moscow that the Kremlin had now become a vast centre for the martial arts with gymnasia, lecture halls, cinemas and auditoriums.

Two days later Michelangelo's sculpture of David in Florence had been transformed so that he was wearing a tuxedo, a top hat and sporting a large moustache, all in pristine white marble. Then Constable's picture of The Hay Wain had been altered so that the cart was up-ended with a broken wheel lying beside it and the hay in the stream.

What was happening? How was it possible for these major works of art to be transformed without the apparent intervention of human hands? The media was in a frenzy of conjecture. Experts, art historians, conservationists, the police and security specialists were all struggling for an explanation, none of which could logically explain the phenomenon. Museums had stepped up their round-the-clock security measures as the trustees were under pressure from all sides. Other famous buildings had also been transformed, mutilated. The White House in Washington had suddenly become an ornate multi-storey car park in bright pink concrete and there were other examples around the world. There was a growing belief amongst the general public that these great achievements of human creativity must have a life of their own. Alien forces were also widely blamed.

Perhaps the strangest happening took place at the British Museum. One section of the Elgin Marbles showing soldiers mounted on horses had now become a procession of riderless horses. The soldiers had disappeared from the frieze leaving a pile of dung and nine one way EasyJet tickets to Athens on the floor of the hall. Urgent enquiries at the airport revealed nothing. Suspicion naturally fell on the Greeks but the authorities there denied all knowledge. On the evening news, the BBC arts correspondent was seen interviewing a government minister with the Acropolis in the background.

On being questioned as to why the Parthenon had been hastily shrouded from view that morning and the whole site closed to the public, the minister replied that urgent and serious faults had been discovered in the structure and that it would need to be closed to the public for the foreseeable future.

Dancer in the Surf

At last John breathed a huge lungful of fresh sea air and then again, a second time. It had been a double period of physics which was always particularly stressful; why on earth do they time-table a double period Friday afternoons he wondered? Giving a long sigh, he had jumped in his car and driven down here just to chill out. Recently, he had been coming here more and more, turning over in his mind whether he should give up his post at the comprehensive all together. Or at least try to go part time, perhaps even get some one-to-one private tuition. But it was the money; at least at the moment he had a regular income from the school and he really needed it to pay off his loan. What to do?

And there was the other matter. His father had died not long ago and it was down to him to clear the house and get rid of a life-time of paperwork. It all had to go so the house could be sold. The prospect was daunting and he preferred not to think about it at all.

At this time of year in the winter, the remote beach was usually deserted; sometimes the odd dog-walker but often he had the place to himself. That's why he liked it. Only the sea gulls which were always there, wheeling in the breeze or strutting across the sand scavenging for a morsel to eat. He scanned the horizon taking in the shore line. Having left his glasses in the car to ease his eyes, all he could make out was a blurred image of someone at the far end a good mile or so away. He looked at the wet sand around his feet, the water draining away as the tide went out leaving ripples on the sand, his foot prints slowly filling with water. Brown strings of seaweed among shells of all shapes and colours strung out along the beach. Nearby was a large pool left behind by the receding tide. In the summer there would be paddling children looking for sea anemones, crabs, urchins and the other treasures of the sea. He could feel himself relaxing as he took in the smell of the salty air. All was just as it should be, he mused, nothing changes. But he knew that things did change, even in the five years since he had been coming. The winter storms had gouged out some of the dunes further along widening the stretch of flat sand. In another five or ten years who knows how wide the beach would be? And in five or ten years, where would he be and what would he be doing?

He started to walk along the beach. The figure he had noticed was moving like a ballet dancer, bending down and then rising to thrust an arm towards the horizon. How wonderful, he thought, to dance here at the water's edge. What a sense of freedom it must give. John lengthened his stride to catch up and as he got closer, he could see it was a young Afro-Caribbean woman and that she was not dancing at all. She was reaching down to the sand, picking up a small object and throwing it out to sea, then walking on a bit further and doing the same again. As he approached, he called out:

"Hi there. Isn't it a lovely day? Can I ask what you are doing exactly?"
She turned, noticing him for the first time. "I'm throwing these starfish back into the sea".

"But why on earth are you doing that?" he asked with a puzzled look on his face.

"Because the tide is going out and if I don't throw them back, they'll die" she replied.

"But there are miles and miles of beach along this coast and there must be dozens if not hundreds of starfish washed up with every tide? You can't possibly make the slightest difference to the starfish population."

She took a few steps and stooped to pick up another one and hurled it as far as she could away from the shore. As it plopped into the water she said

"Well, I made a difference to that one!"

"Hm, you've got a big job on your hands then!"

She turned to look straight at him.

"When my parents came over from Jamaica sixty-odd years ago, they had a really tough time; my Dad committed suicide eighteen months ago, two years after my mother had done the same. It doesn't come much harder than that, I can assure you. I'm still coming to terms with it but my brother and I swore that we would always support each other and do our level best to achieve what our parents wanted for us. We would always be there for each other and although he is working up in Newcastle, I speak to him on the phone every day and share each other's lives. One thing Dad always said was that if you want to make a difference in life, you have to live the change you want to see. I've always been fascinated by the whole process of life so that's why I am studying evolutionary biology and conservation at university. It's fascinating but I've come to realise that all the information we learn is only of limited use. It's what you do with it that matters and that's why I am throwing these starfish back in the sea so they can live a bit longer".

"Wow, that's some undertaking!"

"I don't know why I'm telling you this. Normally I keep it to myself but sometimes it's easier to tell a complete stranger, someone you are unlikely to meet again. I've no illusion that by throwing starfish back in the sea, I am altering the progress of evolution. Perhaps I should join a conservation protest group, campaigning and going on demos. It's just not my style. I often have this argument with my science friends at uni. There is a whole department there studying cosmology trying to understand the big bang, the nature of dark matter and the rest. And there are other universities around the world doing the same thing. To me, it seems like a complete waste of money and more importantly, a waste of top human brain power. If the scientists ever find the answer, what difference will it make? A Nobel prize probably and inflated egos, but will it benefit mankind in any other way? Today, we have far more urgent problems to solve right here on Earth. How are we going to survive the next 100 years and beyond? Trying to solve that is what we should concentrate on and put all our effort and resources into."

John stood stock still and then turned to gaze at the receding waves. Of course, he thought, she's right. I know what I want to happen. I just need to get on and do it. It's the weekend ahead so I've got two whole days to clear out Dad's stuff or at least most of it. And next week, I can do some serious research as to how I can move on from the school. I've always wanted to live abroad; perhaps I could teach English on a one-to-one basis. I'd like that. The penny had dropped. Glancing towards the woman, she had already walked on so he turned, striding purposefully back the way he had come. Just before he left the shore line, he spotted a star fish and stooping to pick it up, threw it with all his might far out to sea.

Liza

Jim kept on plodding up the footpath telling himself I'll pause for a break at the church on the top of the hill. He could then squeeze into the shadow of the church wall to get out of the burning sun and take a good swig of water from his bottle. Having started out straight after breakfast, he had already made good progress along the path along the top of the caldera. It had been uphill all the way so he was looking forward to a pause before continuing upwards again. He thought to himself, it's strange but I've been walking for nearly two hours now and haven't seen a single lizard. Surely there must be lots around here.

-Yes, there came a rasping voice from close behind him. He turned to see who it was but there was nobody in sight.
-Down here, right by the big stone.
Jim looked down but all he could see was a large lizard. I'm sure I heard a voice but there's only a lizard here.
-That's right, only a lizard. The voice was coming straight from the small animal on the edge of the path a few feet away; a rough male voice with a distinctly Greek-sounding accent.
I don't believe this. Am I hallucinating in all this heat?
-No, you are not hallucinating as you call it.
-Just a minute, are you saying you can not only talk and understand what I am saying but also read my mind? How can that be possible? Jim gasped.
-That's right. You humans think you're so clever but there's so much you don't even know that you don't know.

-But how is that possible? Most animals can make noises but no one has been able to converse with one! This is crazy, thought Jim.

-No, it's not crazy; you are talking to me now aren't you? Only a very few of us lizards have this talent but you see, we have been on this earth for a very long time and so have had plenty of opportunity to learn. You humans, how long have you lot been around? Just a drop in the ocean of time and if I'm not mistaken with the way things are going at the moment, we're going to be here long after you lot have gone into extinction.

-That's a cheerful thought! Do you have a name?
-Yes, I am Liza to my friends. And you?
-Liza, is that short for Elizabeth?
-No, no, no. That's a girl's name! Can't you see, I'm a male. Liza is short for Lizard.
-Sorry, I'm not used to talking to lizards. My name is Jim. But tell me how come you can talk to me in English?
-Oh it's not only English. I can understand and talk lots of languages. We get so many people walking along this path so I just tune in as they are passing. After a few languages it becomes easier to learn a new one, although I have to say that I'm struggling a bit with Chinese. I like a challenge though and there's not much else to do up here. Well, it's been nice talking to you but I'm off to hide; I can hear a foursome coming and I don't like the look of them. I wouldn't put it past one of them to try and tread on me; I've had some narrow squeaks in the past. Anyway, have a nice day. Bye.

Jim turned and slowly made his way towards the church. Finding a spot in the shade, he took out his water bottle and had a long swig.

-They'll never believe me when I tell them back home.

Museum Moaner

All the time the museum is open, I have to stay stock still. I daren't move at all, otherwise it would give the game away and there would be such an uproar. Humans think that we statues are supposed to be inert and immovable so as to maintain the fiction that the marble we are carved from is lifeless. This of course is nonsense. True, we are firmly fixed to the plinths we stand on. But after dark when the place is shut and all the lights are switched off, we can all stretch our arms and legs, move our aching backs and rotate our yawning heads. We can also whisper to each other.

You have no idea how tedious it is, day after day, having to listen to these smart-assed tour leaders, so-called experts, telling their groups all about us. When we were carved, who by and for whom, where the marble came from, where we were displayed etc, etc. I am described as the finest sculpture of ancient antiquity. Of course this is true but I have to be careful not to let my chest swell with pride; such a movement would cause endless trouble for all of us. After dark I have learned to remain aloof from the snide remarks of nearby colleagues who miss no opportunity in trying to take me down a peg or two.

I usually try to think back to those days when I was a block of stone in a marble quarry just waiting to be put to some use. One day, the leading sculptor of the time came looking for a suitable piece to start a major commission and, of course, he chose me. After a lot of squabbling about the price and the logistics of moving me, I ended up in his workshop. Soon he started chipping away at my edges using a hammer and chisel. It hurt terribly but that is the lot of a statue. If you want to become something beautiful that people will admire, you have to put up with the pain. It must be a bit like childbirth, very painful but ultimately leading to a wonderful result. And a wonderful male statue is just what I became. The king himself came to inspect me and he was obviously well pleased. Soon I was moved to the city and mounted on a large plinth in a prominent position in the royal palace, no less. Visiting dignitaries and experts drooled over my naked body, its realism, its grandeur, its perfection. Right from the start, I knew I had to remain perfectly motionless. This was not at all easy I can tell you, me without a stitch of clothing in front of the beautiful young women of the city!

But it all went pear shaped when the invaders ransacked the city. They were barbarians and unceremoniously ripped me from my plinth and bundled me onto a ship along with a lot of other statues and treasures and destined for who knows where. We did not get far as a violent storm over-whelmed the laden ship and we all ended up on the sea bed. There we all lay for ages.

I lost track of all time until a man in a diving suit discovered us. Soon we were hauled to the surface and carted off to this museum to dry out. It was a great relief to be cleaned up and to get rid of all those barnacles and stuff that had accumulated on my surface. Before long I found myself in pride of place in this museum where I am now. OK, I accept it's better than lying on the sea bed but I could really do without all the gawping crowds day after day. Still, I suppose if you are the finest statue in all of antiquity, you just must put up with it.

The Musician

He slung the bag with his violin and clothes onto his back and set off again along the road. It was getting late now and he was keen to reach the next town before dark. It had already been a long day and his blistered feet were hurting; the thought of being able to slump on a bed at the khan urged him on. Many of the stones had been removed and used for buildings and walls leaving a deeply rutted path but this part was roughly cobbled, part of the old Roman road. His grandfather had told him that it led from the coast in the far west all the way to Constantinople in the east. Not that he had been any further than the surrounding towns and villages.

He hummed one of his favourite tunes, its rhythm keeping time with his paces. The light was beginning to fade as the sun neared the horizon; it had been a hot and dusty day and the thought of a cool drink of water spurred him on. The land all around him was flat, some of it cultivated but much of it wild with only a distant herd of goats to attract the eye. Glancing over his shoulder, he saw what looked like a distant caravan of asses coming along behind him. It made him quicken his pace as he wanted to get to the khan before them to be sure and get a bed for the night. The khan was popular with travellers who came from far and near. It had dormitories for the men and stabling for the asses and horses with food for all of them.

Tomorrow he would be playing at the home of a wealthy farmer whose daughter was getting married. He was much in demand in the region for the music he could coax from his violin; that was how he made a living. He knew what tunes to play to get people dancing and usually got something extra on top of his fee. The celebrations would go on through the night and into the following day so a good night's rest tonight was just what he needed.

There was always the possibility of robbers along the way. It was not unknown for whole caravans to be ambushed, the wares stolen and even the muleteers slaughtered. Luckily this stretch was open and the robbers usually lay in wait in the passes further on; but you never know. Shuddering at the thought he turned his attention to his fiancée who was waiting back at the village. They wanted to get married and if things turned out well, this glenti would just about give him enough to settle down and start a family. He felt he was getting too old to be wandering round the countryside to earn a living; he could settle down and help his brother-in-law on his farm.

Soon he could see the town he was making for and even from a distance it was obviously crowded with travellers. Making straight for the khan, he had to negotiate with the landlord for a bed for the night and was lucky to get one. Not having had anything since he had left home that morning, he joined the crowd and sat on a bench at a long table to eat the day's meal. Most of the others were drinking wine or beer but he stuck to water; he needed a clear head for what would certainly be a long day and night tomorrow.

Emptying his plate, he got up and went outside to get a breath of fresh air before turning in. In the light of a clear moon, he looked at the surrounding buildings. In front of the khan was the main church which he knew from previous visits and right opposite was a mosque, one of several in the town. He also knew that there was a synagogue nearby in the Jewish quarter although he had not seen it. Whenever he came here, he was struck by the thought that the communities of the three faiths had existed side by side in relative harmony for generations. Situated on this busy east-west road the town had flourished thanks to the requirements of commerce. Apart from the local inhabitants, there were travellers from lots of foreign parts. From the hubbub in the dining room, he had overheard three different languages but he had no idea where they came from. And with that thought, he headed upstairs to the dormitory and was soon fast asleep.

With all the noise and bustle he awoke next morning, had a wash and a bite to eat before leaving the khan. He was not expected at the village until later so for a couple of hours he wandered round the town, making his way down to the river. He fell into conversation with a couple who were also going to the wedding, the man being a relative of the bridegroom. The three of them took the path out of town and walked up to the village. It was obvious this was a wealthy family wedding; the square was filled with tables and chairs, flowers were everywhere and ornate embroidered drapes hung from the facades of the surrounding houses. What you can do when you have got plenty of money, he thought. Good, this should be a nice pay day for me, and he went to make himself known to the bride's father, the man who was going to pay him.

The village filled with arriving guests who mingled with the villagers. Soon the bells rang, summoning everyone to the church where they all piled in, the women on one side of the aisle, the men on the other. An anxious-looking groom waited outside for the bride, accompanied by her father, to arrive and then all three walked slowly down the aisle to where the priest was waiting for them. The familiar wedding service progressed until the priest pronounced them man and wife. Rice and confetti was showered on the couple as they walked amongst the congregation to begin their married life together. At the exit of the church, guests congratulated the new couple and their parents before being given delicate bags of sugared almonds. The waiting tables in the square were now piled with food and people sat down to eat. The musician had been joined by a couple of colleagues to form an impromptu band and soon the sound of the clarinet mingled with his violin while the drummer kept the rhythm. The tunes were all familiar and people joined in with the words of their favourites. Soon a space had to be cleared so that the dancing could begin.

Much later, long after nightfall, the band was able to take enough of a break to have a bite to eat, a drink and a cigarette. Those men who had got up to dance were pleased not to feel obliged to have to show their prowess yet again, at least until the music re-started. Eventually, light began to show on the eastern horizon and those who had remained began to disperse, some to their houses in the village, a few others heading back down the footpath to the town.

Packing away their instruments, they made their way to see the brides' father to get their payments. Looking both elated and tired, the father said how delighted he was with the whole glenti. The three musicians said their goodbyes to each other before setting off, the clarinettist and the drummer hurrying on ahead to join friends making for the town in the opposite direction. Our violinist followed more slowly, feeling well pleased with himself but wondering if he really wanted to give up his life as a travelling musician and settle down. Yes he wanted to marry and have his own family but he did enjoy the freedom of the road, the music and above all, making people happy.

Watermelon

"… and can you buy a watermelon?" Elena said. "They're so heavy, I can't manage it". She folded her arms and glared at Ilia.

"Why do you want a watermelon?"
"…because Kyria Mouropoulos asked for one. She heard the man in the truck going round this morning. Don't tell me you didn't hear it".

Ilia had been shaving at the time and the amplified voice bellowing Karpouzia! Karpouzia! through the open window had made him jump and cut himself on the chin.
"Why didn't she say so at the time? I wouldn't have minded that. He doesn't look at me like…"
The man with the watermelon truck reminded him of his father. Not the old man who turned his face away when Ilia told him he and Elena were leaving Georgia and going to Athens to work, but the father of his youth who used to hoist him onto his shoulders as they walked down to the fields.
"Well where were you at the time? I was busy in the kitchen getting her breakfast whilst you were doing Heaven knows what. What do you ever do?"
"You know very well I've tried to get a job, it's not easy. You've got your work permit".
"Well maybe if you made more of an effort to learn the language…" They had been through this argument before.

"How can I shut up in this flat…"

"You could at least try! There'd be more money to send home and I wouldn't have to work so hard, and you won't even help with the shopping!"

When he went to the local grocer's, they looked at him sideways through narrowed eyes that silently said "What are you doing here? You don't belong". Easy to imagine the phone call to the police after he had left. That's probably what had happened previously when he had been arrested; luckily the court had been lenient and let him off as a first offence but with a warning that the next time would result in a stiff prison sentence.

Elena pushed past him, grabbing the shopping bag and list. From the hall, he heard her speaking in Greek to Kyria Mouropoulos but he understood what she was saying.

"I'm just popping out to get the shopping but Ilia's here if you need anything". The bright tone of her voice, in contrast to that of the conversation they had just had, just made him feel more resentful. The front door closed gently and the slap of her slippers on the marble veranda faded.

Back in Tbilisi, she had had an office job when they first got married. Her wages were low barely covering the rent of their tiny flat and then when Anna was born, they realised they had to do something drastic. The demand for unskilled labouring jobs had dried up completely, so he was unable to help financially. People they knew had gone to Greece finding casual work in the black economy. So they decided to do the same. Elena's sister would look after Anna while they worked in Greece and send back what they could.

That was the plan. Elena had struck lucky and soon found a job as a full-time carer with Kyria Mouropoulos, an elderly widow living in a house with spare bedrooms so the two of them could be together under the same roof. With her out-going nature, she soon picked up enough of the language to get by and after a couple of years got a work permit and did some extra cleaning jobs locally. He on the other hand had given up trying to learn Greek or looking for work and spent most of the day in their room, particularly after his run-in with the immigration police. Only after dark did he feel safe enough to go out.

Ilia picked up a knife and started peeling potatoes and prepping some other vegetables. As he turned away from the sink, he spotted a child's drawing in felt pen on the kitchen table. Three figures, two large and one small, stood in front of a house under a vivid yellow sun. Each of them seemed to be holding large slices of a bright pink cake; underneath, in careful Cyrillic script, were the words Mummy, Daddy and Ann.

He was still studying it when Elena came in dumping two plastic carrier bags on the floor and walked out again. When she reappeared she was carrying a bulging string bag with the green striped skin of a watermelon showing through. Ilia put the drawing on the table and took the bag from her. As he turned back, she said, "Maia sent it. There was a letter this morning."

"What does your sister want? More money?" Elena shook her head and looked away. "What then?"

Elena shook her head again. "She's not going to look after Anna any more. She says she will be better off leaving Tbilisi and getting a job of her own. If I can do it, she..." She grabbed the table and rocked to and fro. "She's not going to look after Anna any more."
Ilia hesitated before touching her arm. She turned and pressed her face into his shirt, shaking as she did so.

"What are we going to do? The tears were flowing freely down her cheeks.
"It'll be alright." And before he could stop and consider, he knew the answer. Laughing, he said. "I'll go back home and look after Anna, that's what I can do. And your sister can do whatever she likes."

When Elena had stopped crying and blew her nose, she said "Anna will like that. We won't all be together but it's a start. Maybe I can send a bit more money and we can save".
Ilia took her small hand in his and with the other one, picked up Anna's drawing. "You, me and Anna together again. But why are we all eating pink cake?" She laughed.

"You know what the shops are like back home, you cannot find anything. Then when we came here I wrote and told her about here." She pointed at the string bag. "We're eating watermelon."

Joyce D'Silva

Ethnicity: Irish

Education: Holy Child Convent, Killiney and Trinity College Dublin

Honorary Doctorates: Two (Universities of Winchester and Keele – thank you!)

Claim to Fame: Granddaughter (x3) of The Liberator (Daniel O'Connell)

Good fortune 1: To have been married to jazz guitarist Amancio D'Silva for 31 years and given birth to three children together

Good fortune 2: To have spent most of my working life with Compassion in World Farming

Good fortune 3: To have lived/worked, been married and had children in India

Good fortune 4: To have found Tai Chi and Qigong 30 years ago and still practise them

Good fortune 5: To have been vegan for 47 years, thus reducing my impact on animals and the environment

Good fortune 6: To have good friends with whom to cry, but mostly laugh.

Current project: Writing a book "Animal Welfare in World Religion: Teaching and Practice" to be published in 2023 by Taylor and Francis.

Dear Living Planet

Dear Living Planet
Magma boiling in your core
Your skin of soil heaving with creatures
Insects, worms, bacteria.
Your trees soaring to the skies
And folding over the swamps.
Your oceans cradling endless water
Teeming with life too,
whales, sharks, fishes, crustaceans,
And suffocating plastic.
Your benign climate
Allowing us to breathe and live
Except where we've polluted it.
Your multitude of creatures
Living by your bounty
On your land,
Only taking what they need,
Except for one species.
I apologise, I apologise
For what we humans do
For what I do.
You may not forgive us in the end
Unless we change our ways.
Can we?

Haiku for Trees
And Other Beings

Two beings
the Tree and me
Warm skin, rough bark,
One being.

Stars and suns so far away
I gaze at their light
I don't really know them
Do they know me?

Scarlet cherries on the tree
Bitter, bitter,
Birds only eat them
When the snow comes

Tiny caterpillar on my houseplant
I don't want you there
Out you go
Gently

When the Birds Have Gone

When the birds have gone, the forest will be silent. A leaf may flutter to the ground, the rain will still patter on the leaves. But there will be a great silence. The men will come with their chainsaws and diggers. The trees will fall in splintering cacophony. When the trees have gone, a great emptiness will fill that space. So many beings are forced into migration or homelessness or dying. The rain will fall on soya monocultures, growing cattle, pig and chicken feed or on the mighty cattle themselves who will fill that treeless space, until their heads are severed.

When the jaguars, the monkeys and the ant-eaters have gone, the insects will flourish for a while. But many insects will flee too or get poisoned with chemicals or trampled in the earth. And one day, when the earth struggles for survival and the men have gone, maybe the rains will return, a new greenery will force its way through the brittle soil and new trees will grow.

Maybe after many years, (but who is there to count them now?), a new forest will emerge. Maybe the insects will return, a few birds will breed again, maybe even a refugee monkey or a migrant jaguar will return. But the men and women who cut the forest down with their saws and their trade, their meaty diets, their pension funds and their investments – they will be gone forever.

Whose Lives Matter?

Of course Black Lives Matter. It's only because White Lives have been mattering for so long, to the exclusion of so many black lives, that it's necessary to emphasise the Black Lives. And of course female White and Black lives didn't matter much for centuries – and in many parts of the world, still don't. (13 women a day get murdered in Colombia.) Which made an excellent reason for the women's suffrage movements of the last century and for the 'Me Too!' movement today.

But what does "matter" mean? The movement surely means that black lives should be regarded as of equal importance in all social and political spheres of activity. Black people should have the same educational opportunities as whites, the same right to vote, equal job opportunities, equal access to social or private housing, equal access to health care of equal quality.

In the US, the rich country built upon the backs of slaves and immigrant labour, (and the semi-obliteration of the indigenous peoples), many black people do not have equal access to all these things. Sadly, it's not so long since black people could not sit in the same restaurants as whites, travel in the same part of the bus or go to the same schools or universities. It now may seem extraordinary that it has taken so long to put right these wrongs. But there's obviously a long way to go.

How can a simple body chemical, melatonin, and its unequal distribution within human beings, be at the root of so much injustice and misery? We don't discriminate on the grounds of unequal amounts of serotonin or stomach acids. Maybe because these are hidden inside. And of course if the entire human race were unable to see, maybe we wouldn't discriminate on the grounds of skin colour.

But even as sighted people, discrimination on the grounds of skin colour doesn't seem to be inbuilt in our genetic code. Very young children of different skin tones play happily together. When I ask my young grandchildren about their friends at school or nursery, they never talk of colour – they might say "she keeps her hair in bunches" or "he's really good at swimming" – they don't SEE colour as a factor to be commented on.

So, we "educate" our young people to see differences where they never saw them before – or never thought they MATTERED. With fateful, sometimes fatal, consequences. Last night's News showed a shocking piece of film, taken on a mobile phone by someone in a car in England, which was driven by a black man. The car is stopped by police. We can see the driver asking the policeman (white) why he's been stopped. The policeman answers "Well, you're a black man"....!!

The stop and search figures in the UK and the injuries and killings in the US by white police tell a dreadful tale of institutional prejudice and racism. And of course, depending on where you live, the "colour" prejudice extends beyond black to people with brown-toned skin. Experiments have been done in the UK where two identical CVs have been sent to companies recruiting staff, one signed by a person with a "white" name and one signed perhaps "Mohammed Ahmed". They get treated very differently. Guess which one gets the interview!

What is it that feeds this prejudice, seeing another not as "another" but as "the other"? Does it all go back to survival instincts from our primate ancestors? Shouldn't we, as moral beings, have outgrown that tendency by now? The moral being inside me says we have to go further in the near future and get to see other sentient beings on this earth as "another" not as "the other" too.

But right now, we have to undertake radical reform in policy, law and education to make sure that Black Lives do Matter.

It's a Chicken's Life

A newly hatched chick. They're fluffy, cute and yellow – the stuff of many an Easter card, decoration or cheap kiddies' toy. This is the only stage of a chicken's life when it can evoke a sentimental "Aah!" from a human. Very occasionally you can come across footage of a mother hen with her chicks, wandering freely in an old-fashioned farmyard or outside a simple dwelling in a poorer country. The hen is crucial to the chicks' continued existence as she teaches her chicks what to eat, what to avoid and how to recognise danger. As good parents do... One more "Aah!" allowed.

Now for the reality check. The jungle fowl from south-east Asia, the ancestor of today's chickens, lived happily in light forest, perched on branches at night to be safe from predators and laid two or three batches of eggs a year. The forest floor yielded a multitude of nutritious and tasty foods and plenty of soil in which to have a dust-bath to clean oily feathers.

Over the centuries we domesticated these animals and bred them for desirable characteristics, like laying more eggs more often, or developing meaty bodies.

In the 20th century the poultry flock really became divided into two – the egg-laying flock and the meat flock, the "broiler" chickens. Now, just two companies globally control the genetics of the broiler flock. You will find the same types of birds in a factory farm in Hampshire as in China, as in Germany as in the USA.

The broiler chickens have been bred over the years to get to slaughter weight more and more quickly. (It's obviously more profitable that way, as you can get more batches through your shed in a year.) The average 2 kilo chicken in the supermarket is now only 5-6 weeks old. It bears no resemblance to its day-old self.

This is a big bonus to the farmers and the company which controls their operations and sells them their stock. The downside is the actual life lived by the chicken, all 20,000 of them or more in one shed. The chicks have now been bred to grow so fast that they have huge appetites and feed voraciously on the soya/cereal feed (often laced with antibiotics). The chicks need to eat. But all that fast muscle growth carries a heavy burden. Literally, the chickens' muscles grow faster than the skeleton and the result is a huge amount of lameness as the chickens get bigger. Research has shown that by about 4 weeks of age anything from 27%- 50% of the chickens have gone painfully lame. Others drop dead from "Sudden Death Syndrome", a realistic name for a heart attack; others die from ascites, fluid on the lungs or have to be put out of their misery. This mortality rate of around 5% is built into the profit/loss calculation of the operation.

When their time comes, they are either grabbed by a robotic machine and swept into transport crates or are gathered up by the legs by people employed to do this unsavoury job. Transported to the slaughterhouse, they then may either be yanked from their crates and hung upside down on a conveyor belt which moves on to the electrified water tank. Their heads are dragged through this and the intention is that they are stunned unconscious so they do not feel the pain of the automatic knife as it cuts their throats. Hopefully, they are also dead by the time they are dipped into the scalding tank to loosen their feathers. Alternatively, the chickens may be stunned and likely killed by exposure to a toxic gas mixture prior to throat cutting.

But the really horrible – and to me outrageous – aspect of modern broiler farming is what happens to the so-called "parent" flock, the chickens kept for breeding. Because these chickens have obviously been bred to grow extremely fast (like their offspring), the breeders must find a way to keep them alive much longer than the 5-6 weeks of their progeny. The chickens won't even reach sexual maturity until 18 weeks of age. The solution to slowing down this fast growth - starve them! They are fed just once in 24 hours. Film of these birds shows them going absolutely frantic when the feed starts coming down the conveyor into the shed. Within 10 minutes all the feed has been eaten and the birds, designed by nature to peck and feed almost constantly in natural conditions, must now wait 23 hours and 50 minutes until their next feed!

When Compassion in World Farming took a case against the government on this issue, we lost the case, but the High Court Judge admitted that these breeder chickens are "chronically hungry". Enjoy your chicken leg (taken from the chickens whose other leg was possibly diseased or broken). You can be sure that that is the only time that joy can be associated with the modern factory-farmed chicken.

How to Be

See the sky, enjoy the sunshine, fly with the wind, feel the water, stand on the earth, sleep on the grass, hug the tree, plant a tree, embrace all creatures – and smile.

Honour your ancestors, forgive your parents, thank your parents, love your siblings, adore your beloved, praise your children, love them forever – and smile.

Care for your friends, forgive your enemies, give to the hungry, support the weary, welcome refugees, play with children, believe in the good – and smile.

Work towards justice, campaign for reform, stand tall in your body, be always diligent, understand others, admit your mistakes, add value to the world – and smile.

Paint your picture, write your story, sing your song, practise your yoga, enjoy your Tai Chi, walk in the country, ride your bicycle, take the train, dig your garden – and smile.

Scream only inside, laugh with others, engage with the lonely, embrace the sad, speak your truth, listen to others, be an example, die to yourself, spread joy in the world – and smile.

One Meat and Two Veg? Possibly Not!

Most of us were brought up on meat and two veg, although those old enough to remember rationing, will recall that meat was definitely a treat during those years. Over the last few decades there has been a huge amount of research on the best diets to eat to minimise the risk of heart disease and various cancers.

Some findings are really important. In 2015 the World Health Organisation (WHO) asked a group of the world's best cancer specialists to look at diet and cancer. The group's report, endorsed by the WHO, makes interesting reading. These experts said that processed meat is carcinogenic (can cause cancer). Examples of processed meat include hot dogs (frankfurters), ham, sausages, bacon, salami and corned beef. These foods are particularly associated with colo-rectal cancer.

So that "Full English" breakfast might need a few tweaks! The experts also said that red meat is "probably carcinogenic". Red meat would include beef, pork, lamb etc. Again, the strongest association is with colo-rectal cancer, but red meat may also be associated with prostate and pancreatic cancers. However, it's not just meat and cancer. A new UK study published in March this year came to the following conclusion:

"Higher consumption of unprocessed red and processed meat combined was associated with higher risks of ischaemic heart disease, pneumonia, diverticular disease, colon polyps and diabetes, and higher consumption of poultry meat was associated with higher risks of gastro-oesophageal reflux disease, gastritis and duodenitis, diverticular disease, gallbladder disease and diabetes."

It's pretty clear that for the sake of our own health we should all reduce our meat consumption. But there are other reasons why it's a good thing to reduce the amount of meat in our diets. We are facing a climate crisis. Livestock production is responsible for 14.5% of all the greenhouse gases that we humans produce – slightly more than all transport emissions globally!

Recently a large team of health and climate change experts produced a Report called the EAT-Lancet Report which calls for a Planetary Health Diet, one that's better for us and our planet. It recommends eating no more than 300 grams of meat per week – that would be roughly two pieces of meat the depth of a deck of cards and the size of the palm of your hand. Note, that is per week, not per day!

We are a nation of animal lovers. Sadly, we sometimes fail to extend our compassion to the animals reared in industrial factory farms, who may live out their lives in cages or on concrete floors or in overcrowded sheds. We can all take action to reduce our meat consumption and take care to choose higher welfare meat when we do buy meat. We can look out for labels such as organic, free range or RSPCA assured.

Permanence

In the fairy tale, often after a struggle and grave danger, the innocent (and always beautiful) Princess marries her Prince and they "live happily ever after". Really?!! No mention of quarrels, possible divorce, ill-health and dying - or any other of life's tribulations.

Indeed many, often younger, couples may marry each other, believing in that ancient myth. Then real life intrudes, babies cry all night, jobs may be lost, homes hard to afford – and so the list goes on.

Tell a school assembly of teenagers that smoking will damage their health and lead often to lung cancer and early death - and the lesson passes right over their heads. At that age life is an adventure waiting to be lived. Death is something that happens to grannies and grandads – or the occasional celebrity or pet hamster. As one gets older, the list of loved ones and friends who have died gets longer and longer. It seems there is no passport to permanence.

Older people realise that they too will die. They may not accept this fact but they know it's true. And of course believers in any of the religious faiths may believe that their soul or essence does somehow live on – in a heavenly paradise or by being reincarnated. Some believe that the earth itself will be transformed again into the kingdom of god and all the departed will rise again.

For the non-believer, this is all nonsense. Like all other creatures, humans have material bodies and these will rot in the grave or be cremated and turned to ash. Why are we so determined to avoid annihilation? Do we feel we need another chance to "get it right"? Or, is this the just reward for living life by the book – whichever "book" you follow? Are we frightened of just not being? Do we feel that a continued existence is the only way we can meet again with our departed loved ones, our soul mates?

Are we afraid that if there is no continued existence after death then we may have followed the rules and led a "good" life for nothing – when we could have cheated our way to fame and fortune and enjoyed the delights of multiple extreme sexual experiences which we've never tried but which might have been highly pleasurable. But let's look beyond our self-centred human musings. What of other creatures on earth? If humans, a leading primate species, are subject to life and death and an afterlife, then surely all the other creatures must be entitled to that further existence too? There might be a lot of sheep in heaven! And ladybirds and cockroaches and fish too! (And that wasp outside my window just now…)

What of the earth itself? We may be destroying its surface, its soils and forests and greenery, we may be killing its oceans with carbon and plastic and industrial and agricultural pollution, but could it perhaps be permanent? Sadly, no. The scientists have done their predictions and the blue planet will eventually endure its own cremation. So what are we left with? Can those lovely qualities of compassion and generosity exist without beings to embody them? Probably not.

Although, as they are immeasurable by science, as yet, we cannot be sure that the whole universe of material existence might end and there would just be those qualities left, unembodied, just floating in the ether of non-existence. Prove me wrong!

Heiner Thiessen

My current incarnation started in war-torn Germany in 1942. My parents became refugees soon enough and we had to find a new home amongst the burnt out ruins of Hamburg. Through that early experience I have remained mesmerised by the rise and fall of civilisations. My personal focus on the transience of Empire led me to the Palace of Knossos on Crete where I worked for Bishop Irineaus on an American demonstration farm. Then there was the Library of Alexandria, where Eratosthenes revolutionised our world view, and finally there was the Colosseum in Rome.

It was in the Italian capital that I worked for the Food and Agriculture Organization of the UN, visiting African Fisheries and advising on Sustainable Fisheries Management. Our Sub-Saharan hosts had their own perspectives. Later, when teaching at Portsmouth University we went back to Africa with an agenda of vocational curriculum development at Senegalese Universities.

Later still, I spent time in Senegal and Portugal, no longer trying to tell anybody anything. I had the good fortune to meet my soulmate Diane on a Mennonite demonstration farm on Crete. We had 46 good years together until her spirit flew home. Our creative twin boys have their own fascinating pathways. Now that I am on the wrong side of Eighty, I often wonder where the Karmic Laws will send me next time round.

Of Clouds and Shadows

Thinking for oneself and avoiding any form of hero-worship seems sound advice, and most of my life I have followed it with genuine conviction. But in my quieter years, and closer to the big cliff, where I have found the space and time to live on a sloping ledge, well beyond the realm of grinding necessity, I have discovered a fellow human being with whom I feel great kinship and even a sense of quiet admiration, having none of his outstanding qualities myself.

I am talking about a Greek polymath who had a finger in almost every scientific pie of his day. They called him the pentathlete, due to his mental prowess in so many disciplines. He was a poet, a mathematician, a geographer, an historian, an astronomer, and finally, the director of the most important library of the ancient world, situated in Alexandria on the shores of the Mediterranean Sea in Egypt, west of the Nile Delta. I am talking about Eratosthenes, who was born in North Africa in about 276 BC and who spent most of his adult life in the Greek colony of Alexandria, newly established by the ambitious Macedonian warlord Alexander the Great.

Eratosthenes' long life is crowded with achievement, the best known perhaps his nearly correct calculation of the circumference of the Earth. The pentathlete worked this out without any great technological assistance, or even travelling.

103

Eratosthenes simply sits outside his front door under a perfectly blue sky. He watches the length of shadow of the obelisk in front of his Library in exactly the same way that everybody else can. As the shadow slowly approaches the North South meridian line, that has been beautifully engraved into the sandstone floor, he keeps a piece of charcoal at the ready. And when shadow and engraved meridian line coincide for a short fleeting moment, the astronomer marks the shadow length on this Summer Solstice Day. It should be the shortest noon shadow of the entire year, as the sun reaches its highest altitude on this special date.

Anyone could have done that. Sitting, gazing, waiting and finally marking the floor with a bit of charcoal. The difference between him and all other contemporary observers lies in the fact that he can interpret this shadow with a vivid sense of imagination. The astronomer has the ability to send his mind travelling far into space, as if standing on the surface of the Moon and looking back at Earth from a long distance, so that he can visualise the entire rotund planet in front of his inner eye.

What he sees is simple. He may not have seen our lonely blue globe in the way the crew of the Apollo 11 Mission could look back at their home planet, but he visualises a sphere with a centre. And wherever the sun shines onto this sphere perpendicularly, as it does on Summer Solstice Day onto the Tropic of Cancer (see point S below), its light travels deep into any well that might be located anywhere on this Tropic of Cancer latitude circle. In fact the solar rays would travel in a straight line right to the centre of planet Earth, if the well could be dug that deep. (See point O)

But Eratosthenes is far away from this deep well in Syene. In fact the thinker, still in dreamtime high above our planet, visualises himself near the Nile delta now, in Alexandria on the coast of the Mediterranean Sea, many miles north of that well. (See point A). And he imagines himself at the bottom of the obelisk at noon, observing a shadow. At the same time he remembers from an ancient papyrus scroll in his library, that every year at this Summer Solstice moment, the sun shines deep into a well at Syene on the Upper Nile. The locals had found this remarkable and documented it. He can see all these things clearly with both his eyes firmly shut.

The pentathlete reasons that parallel sun rays reaching the Earth's surface do in fact arrive at different angles. The sun generates no shadow at S and some shadow at A. And with these two simple observations Eratosthenes concludes correctly that the Earth must be round. His ingenuity further constructs a line from A to O. It is the vertical and virtual downward extension of the obelisk, right to the centre of our planet, where two lines now intersect. According to the laws of geometry the resulting angle alpha at the centre O is identical to the angle at the top of the obelisk, defined by the altitude of the sun on this Solstice Day. And that is all. Measure the shadow length and the height of the obelisk, and you can work out the angle alpha at the top of the obelisk, which must by definition be identical to the angle at the invisible and inaccessible centre of the planet. It is elementary Euclidean geometry. Pure Genius.

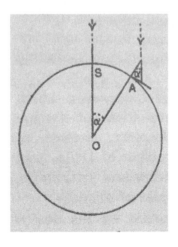

With the angle alpha now in place, which the polymath deems to be close to 7.2 degree, he concludes that this angle fits exactly fifty times into a full circle of 360 degrees. Or in simpler language, there would have to be fifty segments of a virtual orange, to create a complete citrus fruit. And now he can work out the actual circumference of our planet or of our imagined orange. Or can he?

The only missing link in our project is the actual direct surface distance from Alexandria to the well at Syene. Nobody has ever measured the paces from A to S reliably. Not up to then anyway. There was no need to do so, because the Nile flows effortlessly from South to North into the Sea, thus being the superior transport route. Eratosthenes actually commissions a group of geometers to measure this particular distance. We do not know how this was done, or how exact their measurements would have actually been. But we know that the pacers or pedometers came back with tangible results.

They reported that it took their camels fifty days to journey north-south from Alexandria to Syene. And that in itself was invaluable information, because it suggested that, optimistically speaking, one would need a total of at least 50 days x 50 orange segments = 2,500 days to circumnavigate our world on camelback. An expedition could travel around this globe in approximately seven years, if the geography of the planet permitted such a direct line of travel overland and the poor camels never tired on their journey.

Additionally the geometers also inform Eratosthenes that the distance between the obelisk and the well has been estimated as being 800km. The pacers work with units of measurement called 'stadia', the running distance of the oval circumference of a Greek stadium, but the result, translated into modern metrics, looks approximately like the figure above. If you multiply this figure by fifty orange segments, you arrive at the astonishing result of 40,000km. This is an awe inspiring outcome, surprisingly close to modern satellite measurements of the circumference of planet Earth. The latest figure, published by NASA, is 40,070 km. We can only marvel at the ingenuity of an old librarian in North Africa, who had the wit and the presence of mind to size up our entire planet with a bit of tape measure just sitting outside his own home.

In summary, our polymath from Alexandria arrives at three major conclusions, which changed the world forever. First, his experiment tells him that our home planet is in fact a sphere:

When parallel sun rays cast different shadow lengths at different latitudes, our planet must be round. Secondly, he concludes that its circumference is approximately 40,000km, which is close to the actual figure. Thirdly he inspires the world of navigation, suggesting to his contemporaries, but also to the many yet unborn generations following him, that by sailing the 'okeanos' in a westerly direction the sailors would eventually reach home again, now arriving from the east. That idea must have seemed sensational at the time.

Unfortunately, his navigational suggestion was practically forgotten for many centuries. It was certainly not followed up for more than one and a half millennia, until shipbuilding had become far more advanced and the time had come for such a daring ancient challenge to be taken seriously by the likes of Columbus and Magellan. These seafaring explorers knew about Eratosthenes and his famous calculation and with the newly-developed type of maritime vessel, the Iberian Caravela, such a voyage suddenly seemed achievable enough. So they decided to put his ancient and daring hypothesis to the test. The rest is history.

And here is the reason for my fascination with Eratosthenes: if simple shadow watching in antiquity could lead to such amazing conclusions, and many centuries later even to the discovery of new continents, then we have to marvel at the wonders of simple scientific measuring. We also have to be in awe of the mind of a Greek genius who could distill a brand new worldview that changed everything with a very simple, almost mundane observation which all of us could potentially have made, but whose importance apparently only he could appreciate.

We might also ask ourselves how the likes of Eratosthenes would have interpreted the world if a permanent cloud cover would have prevented us all from seeing blue skies, the Sun, the Moon, and of course, the stars. In such a world, shadows resulting from heavenly objects would have been unimaginable. Without measurable shadows, and without observation of the night sky, would we not have had less new knowledge, less scientific advance? Or would the intrinsic curiosity of Homo sapiens have led us in a very different direction of enquiry?

And a further thought flows from this question. Our pursuit of scientific knowledge – perhaps starting with Eratosthenes' humble shadow readings – has taken us to the Moon, to Mars, and well beyond. But we also have to concede that we have not yet progressed very far in other fields of human inquiry. Is it possible that we suffer from some other form of 'cloud cover', disallowing 'shadow readings' in other disciplines? What type of 'shadow mark' are we now incapable of perceiving? What e.g. is consciousness? Where does artistic inspiration come from? Why for example do we still not know what happens to us after death? Why are we not certain about the thoughts and intentions of the great watchmaker in the sky? Why do we end up with competing religions? Generally, what sort of 'cloud cover' do we need to penetrate in order to arrive at a greater understanding of the human condition, with its many questions that so far defy measurement?

Did the Romans have an inkling of this conundrum when they pronounced Lux Umbra Dei Est ('Light is the shadow of God')? Could it be that the truth is a light, perhaps too powerful for the human eye and for man's consciousness? By Eratosthenes' time Plato had already developed his Allegory of the Cave, in which humans are forced to live in the shifting shadows of a cave, held captive, not being equipped for the bright divine light outside – a luminosity, a truth, that would certainly blind us!

And considering imperceptible shadows, should we perhaps also include the world of 'Jungian shadow' at this point – shadows of the mind which we cannot perceive, or prefer not to be aware of, since they are too painful to encounter?

When the great Eratosthenes lost his eyesight at the age of eighty he also seems to have lost his zest for life. Perhaps, in spite of his many brilliant achievements, he yearned for new adventures in unknown realms. As a result, he decided to deliberately move towards the unknown by no longer feeding his human frame, and starving himself into the next world. This was perhaps his final and most daring scientific experiment, expressing his hunger and thirst for light and shadow of a higher order. It is perhaps this last detail of his life that resonates most with me. It highlights the idea of living life to the full and embracing our sojourn here, sometimes under clouds and sometimes under bright blue skies, casting shorter and longer shadows as we move about, encountering truths that we can hardly express in human language because even the shadows are far too bright for us.

The Jacob's Ladder

Being close to her final days but wide awake and fully alert, Marga was ready to talk. I asked her about the highlights of her life. 'Oh, there wasn't much', she came back quietly. 'My life was like living in a penal colony. Das Leben ist ein Straflager'. I shuddered at such stark conclusions. Marga had lived through two world wars. Her family had lost everything twice over, first in the hyperinflation of 1923 and then again in January 1945, when the Red Army approached fast.

But do you remember any events that stand out in your long life? With great clarity and wonderful calm Marga explained: 'When the Russian Army stood at the gates of Eastern Prussia and we were finally given permission to leave our homes by order of the High Command in Berlin, it was by then the 27th of January and ice cold winter weather had descended. Minus twenty degrees centigrade were quite normal for January. The roads were completely congested with horse drawn carriages, hopelessly overloaded with belongings which their owners could not possibly do without, or so they erroneously assumed. Everyone was headed for Danzig, the historic Hanseatic Seaport. When we left our home, we decided that we needed to get to a smaller port, hoping for evacuation by some rescue vessel before the Red Army would reach those coastal places. All roads to Danzig were chockablock by now and the only shortcut to the Coast was over the frozen Lagoon, the 'Frische Haff'.

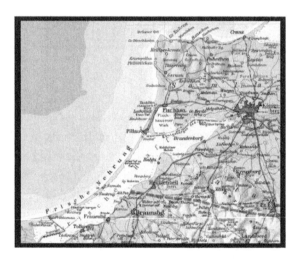

Like in all winters, the lagoon was covered in thick ice and snow. One minute you were on land, the next you were on ice without even knowing the difference. Thousands of people from all over Eastern Prussia were trekking over the winter lagoon day and night, hoping to reach the Baltic seaport of Pillau.

Marga continues in her matter of fact account, devoid of any emotion: 'My mother and I were walking across the ice. We had no carriage, no horses, we were poor. Both of us were weighed down with heavy rucksacks holding all our worldly belongings.

My mother was in her seventies, physically unwell and totally unfit. But I saw her summoning all her strength, walking uncomplainingly with the trek without ever falling behind. We saw overloaded horse drawn carriages suddenly breaking into the splitting ice and sinking rapidly in the dark of night, people and horses drowning, without anybody stopping to help. It was mere personal survival that was on our brains. The ice could break anywhere and at any moment with all these people crossing the lagoon and fleeing their ordinary lives to have an outside chance of staying physically alive.

When we got to the port of Pillau, people were told that there was no space for coaches and horses aboard ship. There was no gangway either. Just a rope ladder up the steep side of a tall freighter, docking against tractor tyre fenders, thus creating a considerable gap from hull to pier that seemed frightening and potentially lethal. It was the most amazing and awe inspiring thing I can remember of all the things that happened in my life, that my ailing mother in her mid seventies and burdened with a heavy backpack managed to cross the yawning quayside gap and climb the Jacobs Ladder in icy conditions, rung by rung up to the ship's frozen railing. Not everybody made it to the top. Those who fell, would hit the quay or drown mercilessly without any chance of help in the black waters between quay and ship. I shall never forget. When it really matters, human nature craves nothing but survival.

Miraculously, we both made it to the top and we were able to stay on the icy deck for three days and nights without being torpedoed or bombed by Russian aircraft on our voyage to the West. Not all ships were that fortunate. Had we decided to walk to Danzig, we might not have been so lucky. The cruise liner 'Wilhelm Gustloff' e.g. was sunk on the 30th January 1945 with an estimated 9,400 passengers losing their lives in the icy Baltic Sea after a Soviet torpedo, fired from a submarine, struck the hull of the elegant passenger ship just west of Danzig. It was the greatest naval catastrophe in maritime history. But it was soon forgotten, because we are a defeated and dishonoured nation. When the Titanic sank 1,517 lives were lost.

Marga is pleased to have a listener. Finally we all landed in Denmark, because Germany was out of bounds for us. The British stopped all refugee influx from Denmark because too many houses were in ruins and there was just no shelter anywhere.

By now Marga is in full flow. 'In our Danish camp we had almost nothing and yet we had everything at the same time.' We had all survived and suddenly we were all equals. Nobody had more than they could carry with their own two hands. And Marga smiles and looks younger all of a sudden. We had to stay in Denmark in this refugee camp for three years. They were the best years of my life. The camp was full of talent and we ran courses and had choirs and an orchestra. I taught shorthand because I had worked as a secretary. We had to organise everything ourselves. The food, the cleaning, the laundry. It was primitive but we were not spoiled and grateful for our survival.

Marga was my father's second wife. He remarried after our mother had died. She seemed an outwardly unassuming person one could easily overlook. But Marga was full of resolve and quiet wisdom and made us understand that climbing a Jacob's Ladder with a heavy backpack on an icy January's night could be easily achieved, when the need actually arose, even when you are old and frail. We are always stronger than we think.

Marga died some twenty years ago and even my adult sons still talk about her with respect and with quiet admiration. Her spirit lives on, climbing that ladder to Heaven forever more.

A Catch too Far

There is clearly no way of knowing, but doesn't it seem likely that early Sapiens caught his very first fish with his own two hands? After all, this is what mammals and birds had been showing him forever. But we can also assume with some certainty that such a simple 'un-tooled' approach would soon have been replaced by a wittier tactic of the 'knowing new man'. Sapiens' brainy ingenuity would soon lead him to arrive at a variety of labour saving options. One fine day he would discover spearfishing. Then he would dream up the fish trap and later the fishing net. The improved food supply chain, resulting from such advances, would allow his family to grow. He, who had the nous, could multiply. Natural selection favoured inventiveness.

Progress through smart thinking, as opposed to brute force, has been Sapiens' trade mark for thousands of years in all areas of life and that includes the domain of fishing. But there came a point in the human success story, when his own ingenuity would eventually catch up with him (pun intended) and begin to imperil the world around him. In fact, Sapiens himself seems to have become the victim of his own ingenuity.

Overfishing leads to dwindling maritime stocks and thus to loss of livelihood in the fishing communities. If we don't act in harmony with nature all around us, Mother Earth will let us know in no uncertain terms. When we eat the raft we are sailing on, we are in deep trouble.

One sunny afternoon in West Africa I found myself in the eye of a perfect storm that had resulted from such an aggressive technology that proved far too successful for its own good. My own physical safety that afternoon was no longer a foregone conclusion.

West African fishing in the wild waters of the Atlantic Ocean is not for the faint hearted. The picturesque pirogues on the wide beaches of Saint Louis don't make you think of death and drowning. And yet fishermen fail to return regularly. The seas are unpredictable and the fishermen don't usually know how to swim. From a European perspective most of the crew members I saw on any pirogue seemed far too young. Ten year old children crew the boats, together with fathers and older cousins. Pushing a long and narrow pirogue through the powerful surf, out into the open waters and jumping aboard at the last possible moment, completely soaked by then, is a spectacle I shall never forget. No health and safety there. No worried mothers either, concerned for the boys who will be away for days and nights with the weather beaten men.

Several days later, when the pirogues return, the beach is crowded with excited women, glad to see their menfolk and their sons all back alive. They argue about the best fish, what part of the catch will be cooked at home, and what goes to market. Fish is a staple diet in West Africa. 'Djeb bu Jen', fish and rice is on the menu almost every single day, a beautifully spiced source of protein and very tasty to the palate. I never grew tired of it.

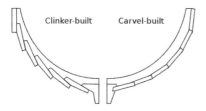

Fishing by Pirogue has been practised for centuries. But it was first made possible, when the Portuguese and the Spanish arrived with their new ideas of 'carvel' boat building, featuring rib frames and edge on edge planking, thus replacing the stone age dugout canoes which capsized far too easily and which were more suited for river and lagoon fishing, away from the dangerous breakers and the forbidding Atlantic surf.

Technological progress in Caravella shipbuilding, originating from the Iberian Peninsula did not only facilitate the great trans-Atlantic voyages of exploration, the new Pirogue of Iberian origin also opened up oceanic fishing grounds and allowed coastal populations to feed sustainably from a rich harvest that the wild sea offered. To this day, the construction and the colourful decoration of the African pirogue is surprisingly similar to the Portuguese boats I spotted on the canals of Aveiro, where they were called Piroga.

Aveiro, Portugal

But nothing lasts forever and what was cutting edge technology many centuries ago, will eventually be overtaken by new developments. First came the outboard motor, granting the local fishermen a wider radius of action and thus a richer harvest. A generation later, Factory Trawling with sonar tracking of fish stock movement, began to intrude and jeopardise traditional subsistence fishing in West Africa. No alarm bells rang when the first trawlers from China and Korea arrived on the West African coast with its rich fishing grounds. They would harvest local mackerel, herring and mullet, then process, package and freeze their catch, ready to be marketed in Europe and Asia.

Their trawlers would initially operate outside territorial waters, or later, with ministerial fishing permits, ever closer to the shore. Eventually local fishermen began to feel the pinch of high tech overfishing. They caught less and less. Sorties were no longer viable and fish became more and more expensive, if not a luxury product. The fishing community had been deprived of their own local natural resource by a superior, yet predatory technology from far away.

Like everywhere else, the machine had finally won. Traditional man was at the losing end of this global Productivity Drive. He had to rethink his own business model. His beached pirogue could no longer pay off his rising debt, nor could it feed hungry mouths. So the idle and desperate crews took their boats out into the Atlantic, further out than they had ever done before to offer their services to the new masters with their avaricious technology. Their own pirogues would be tied to the trawlers. And the crews would stay aboard ship for a while, working on the gutting tables, assisting with packaging and freezing, before the freight would finally be shipped to Europe from Dakar.

It is tough work and accommodation is damp and primitive but the lads are happy to have a job at all and to take their share of the catch home or to market. This practice has been going on for decades and at least since the beginning of this 21st century. Territorial waters have to be fiercely guarded with small aircraft, reporting on intrusion, so that offending companies can be fined accordingly.

One day, while I was in Saint Louis, rumour spread like wildfire through the entire country that neighbouring Mauritanian trawlers had strayed into Senegalese waters, protected by their two hundred mile economic exclusion zone. The news worked like the proverbial match igniting a tinderbox. Feelings had been running high for ages. Fishermen were on edge. Not everyone got a job with the Chinese and Korean trawlers. And now, even the Mauritanians began to stray illegally into their Senegalese fishing grounds. 'It always seemed to be the Mauretanians, causing trouble for the locals, especially here, so close to the National border.

Mauritanian immigrants ran the shops in town. They were better at commerce in general. Import and export businesses were in their hands. They were richer and owned some of the hotels and the restaurants. Envy loomed large and hatred, directed at these successful foreigners was tangible. When rumour about the offending boats from across the border struck the town of St. Louis, all hell broke loose. Mauritanian shops were looted, shop owners were attacked and killed, although they had nothing to do with the rumoured fishing activities of their compatriots. It was the nearest to pandemonium I have ever come across.

And there I was in my taxi, going back to my hotel after a day's work at University. When crossing the Senegal River our vehicle approached a large group of angry fishermen. It was too late to reverse or turn the car around to take a different route. We were caught amidst agitated and excitable men who needed an outlet for their frustration. They hated foreigners. I was a foreigner. Did their anger extend to Europeans in suits? There was no way of knowing. The taxi driver told me to smile. We heard hands banging on the top of the roof from all sides, as the driver inched his way forward. Nobody stopped us but the drumming on the car top intensified, now accompanied by some aggressive chanting. The looting was still in full swing and a general sense of lawlessness hung in the air. It could have ended in tears but mercifully and very gradually we were allowed to leave the unruly mob behind. A Mauretanian passenger may not have fared quite so well.

Industrial overfishing, organised by factory trawling companies from the Far East had suddenly intersected with my own little life. This seemed ample proof of the validity of Chaos Theory that everything is in fact interconnected with everything else. It also made me think how easily a technology can turn inappropriate and damaging, particularly to those who are weak and voiceless. But often enough we only wake up when it is already far too late.

Have we bought the benefit of improved living standards and rising life expectancy at a price that cannot be paid forever? Are a growing world population and looming climate change an expression of man made imbalances within nature? Have we caught that one fish too many?

The Writing on the Wall

It was only a few days into the Second World War. So far, it had consisted of nothing more than what the 'Voice' on the radio called the Polish Campaign. 'Germany had to resort to retaliation for the Polish attack on the Radio Station Gleiwitz'. Could one believe the Voice? Could one afford to harbour poisonous and treacherous forms of doubt in one's heart? Perhaps that lack of confidence in political leadership could become outwardly visible over time. Hearts were heavy everywhere. Where would it all end? Another Versailles?

Albert was in his early fifties by now. He and Elsa led frugal lives on the third level of a six floor apartment block in Frankfurt on the River Main. No hot water, no bathtub. A newfangled radio with one single station.' Volksempfänger'. The voice of Truth.

Albert and Elsa are afraid whenever the doorbell rings, especially after dark. They are afraid whenever the postman knocks at the door. They have not heard from Helmut for ages. He was only 18 when he left home. A boy really. But after the first wave of Anti Jewish Pogroms on the 9th November 1938, when the Synagogues all over the country went up in flames and the Jewish shop fronts were ransacked with broken glass everywhere, their tiny world had changed forever. All their hopes and all their self-deceiving optimism, that it could not possibly ever come to this, had now been shattered, literally.

Synagogue Berlin November 1938

They had been too credulous, too gullible, first of all, too unimaginative to even consider the possibility of orchestrated mass aggression against their own kind. The warning signs though had been there all along but then every one of these individual events had been too painful, too frightening and too breathtaking, each of them in their own right. There was no mental space left for Albert to link and join together all of these occurrences to form a wider, bigger picture. It had been so much easier to look the other way, to focus on their everyday challenges, instead of seeing the gradually rising tide of hostilities and chicanery against the people of Mosaic origin, even if they had been secular and culturally German, and like Albert, serving their Kaiser Wilhelm during WW1. Now, none of it made any difference at all.

Now, they all fell under the jurisdiction of the Nuremberg Race Act of 1935, an outrageous Law compartmentalising people into all sorts of new categories from Full Jew to

Halfcast Second Degree. It also robbed them of their Citizenship and turned them into tolerated outsiders. The new Law had cost Albert his clerical job at the Council Offices. But he soon found new work at a private company through friends of friends. Everyone needed accountants and not everyone supported this regime. Albert and Elsa had to produce family trees now, three generations back, so that they could be classified accordingly. Albert and Elsa were 'Full Jews'. And so was their only son Helmut.

But when the Night of Broken Glass led to Jewish fatalities and 30,000 deportations of Jewish males to concentration camps, life had changed irretrievably. Critical mass had been reached. Even if his parents felt too old and too disconnected from the world beyond, Helmut at least had to leave, the sooner the better. One fine day in November 1938 Albert and Elsa took their 18 year old son to Frankfurt Hauptbahnhof, walked up platform Six and waved him goodbye. He smiled unconvincingly and showed them his ticket to Amsterdam through the dirty window of his railway compartment. They had not heard much since that day.

It was ten months ago now and they had only ever received one standard postcard from London, issued by the Red Cross, confirming Helmut's safe arrival in his new world across the Channel. Albert and Elsa had hoped for much more information. But the world was not like that.

At the beginning of 1939 another new Law comes into force. All Jews need to have first names, deemed to be typically Jewish. New parents have to choose from a prescribed list of limited choice. Jewish adults have to add 'Israel' or 'Sarah' to their first names. It is the beginning of unashamedly earmarking the victims for the Final Solution. But life goes on and no noisy alarm bells seem to be ringing for Albert and Elsa.

And then on the 10th September 1939, ten days into WW2, the postman delivers an official looking letter in a bland green envelope with a German stamp. The heart rate rises, even before Albert-Israel tears open the envelope. It is from the Head of the Jewish Community in Frankfurt. The document looks cold and hostile and Albert-Israel and Elsa-Sarah can't understand what it says. So many complicated words, so many legal terms. But they reason that the letter is from the Synagogue. It can't possibly be bad or threatening. Surely, they are all of the Tribe of Jacob, even if Albert-Israel and Elsa-Sarah don't attend Synagogue in their modern agnostic ways of thinking. When the heart rate descends gradually and the mind calms a wee tiny bit, they both sit down at their kitchen table, with Albert reading the Letter back to Elsa, slowly and clearly.

Statistical Census of the entire Jewish Population for Official Purposes

It is the duty of all members of the Imperial Union of Jews in Germany, to complete the enclosed questionnaires with full attention to detail, and to submit these without delay. The forms are to be completed and submitted by return of post and at the latest by Monday, 2nd October 1939 to the Office of the Jewish Parish in Frankfurt, Friedrichstraße 29. The statistical census of the entire Jewish population must be updated and completed immediately. As this statistical survey serves official purposes, the Office of the Jewish Parish declines all responsibility for late or nil submissions.

A list of instructions follows, detailing the inclusion of each single person of the household, their economic status, their assets and valuables. Separate questionnaires are required for each child. The leaflet is signed by the Head of the Jewish Community in Frankfurt/Main.

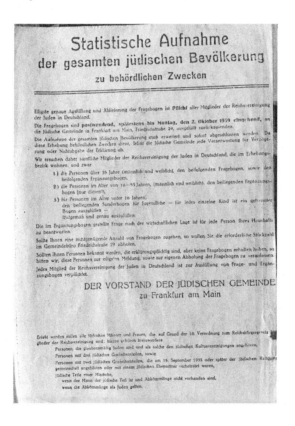

Statistische Aufnahme
der gesamten jüdischen Bevölkerung
zu behördlichen Zwecken

Albert and Elsa fill in the enclosed forms diligently and obediently, not just for themselves but also for absent Helmut. They do not want to alert officialdom to the fact their son is no longer in Frankfurt. The warning lights in Albert's household however are still not coming on. They are law-abiding folk. Always have been. They don't pack their bundles and disappear into the night. They do not go into hiding. Their imagination does not include resettlement programmes, ethnic cleansing and long journeys in windowless goods trains. They simply cannot imagine that anything untoward could ever happen to them. The Law of Inertia does not only apply to Physics.

They carry on with their little lives until, eventually, they receive yet another letter, instructing them to meet at the local railway station at 2:00 in the morning with one single suitcase per person. And they still don't go into hiding or start an uprising. They arrive on time at the appointed hour. Their conditioning is so powerful that all else would seem disobedient and disrespectful of an almighty and all knowing state.

Albert and Elsa board a goods train that takes them from Frankfurt to Theresienstadt, Terezin, north west of Prague in Bohemia. They arrive at a concentration camp, open to occasional international inspection with its own orchestra and the odd concert. But it is also a hub for other destinations that afford none of these niceties. And so, inevitably, Albert and Elsa obediently board yet another windowless goodstrain to one of those other places with their unspeakable names, where they finally perish without any trace of a written record of their demise.

Shortly after the outbreak of WW2, 19 year old Helmut, by now in London, is classified as an Enemy Alien and sent to live in a huge sports stadium somewhere in the UK until he and thousands like him are shipped from Liverpool to Canada. He is lucky because his ship is not bombed and sunk by the Luftwaffe. He spends several winters under canvas. When I meet him in 1976, he has anglicised his name. The past had been just too painful.

Did he ever go back to Frankfurt, I ask. He takes his time to reply, perhaps pondering whether I am worthy of a truthful answer. Twenty years after the war, Helmut receives a letter on headed paper from the Town Council of Frankfurt. They invite him to go back to his home town for a 'Gathering of International Reconciliation'. All expenses paid generously. Helmut travels to Frankfurt and joins in the proceedings of this international event with concerts, speeches, discussions and the emotional meeting of old acquaintances. Towards the end of his time there, he is invited to the Town Hall, where a clerk hands him a large brown envelope, containing some of his parents' belongings. He finds the postcards and letters he had sent from London and Canada that had never reached his mum and dad. He finds letters from relatives who had made it to Holland and cryptically reported about the arrests of uncles and cousins. The Red Cross issue postcards prescribe a maximum of words and are open to official scrutiny. 'Uncle Ernst and Auntie Martha have gone on a journey'.

He finds his parents' wedding certificates, his own birth certificate and a Letter issued by the Head of the Jewish community in Frankfurt, requesting prompt cooperation with a government that had already taken away their citizenship, their right to work in the public sector, their names and finally their very own son.

Helmut has told me all this. He was a good friend of mine at Portsmouth Polytechnic. When he retired, he quietly handed me a brown envelope. It contained a photocopy of a letter from the Head of the Jewish Community in Frankfurt. It seemed no more than an insignificant leaflet.

Toby

The WhatsApp ping always sounds deeply satisfying to me. How did they manage to engineer such an appealing ringtone? I open my iPhone and there it is: The new chat message. It is from someone whose details I don't recognise and who is not amongst my listed contacts. I only see a number and a blurred Photograph of a seemingly unknown face. How did they get hold of my number? Have I been spammed? Even on WhatsApp now?

'Hello Heiner, how are you today?'
'Who are you?'
'It would be good to talk'
'Who are you?'

'I have been looking after you for a very long time. I am from the 'Personal Security Department'. Your grandparents would have been familiar with the term 'Guardian Angel', but that sounds a bit 'old hat' if not outright embarrassing these days.'

'What do you want? I can block you.'

'Don't be rash. You remember Northwick Park Hospital 2001, where you almost died? I was there looking after you when they rolled you into the Operating Theatre.'

'What d'you mean?'

'You were clearly on the way out after that long flight under that oxygen mask.'

'How do you know all this? What are you trying to sell?'

'When they drained your liver with those long syringes while you followed the proceedings on the monitor, it was all touch and go. I helped the surgeon then and steadied her hand. You are here because the OP went well.'

What is this? Some new algorithmic cyber attack? The totalitarian side of our new digital civilization is truly frightening. The things they know about you! Its invasiveness is quite unsettling. I delete the contact, blocking the fraudster. Within minutes it pings once more, this time from a different number. Same blurred photograph.

'Hallo Heiner. Here is your Guardian Angel again.'

'There are no such things as Guardian Angels, get real man.'

'Remember the ruins of Hamburg when you climbed to the fourth floor of this bombed-out shell of a building and you jumped from iron girder to iron girder, with an open drop four floors deep? You were only eight.'

My hair stands on end. Nobody would have known about my nipper days in war torn Hamburg. At least not here in the U.K. Could this be real? Just potentially? My brain goes blank and my mouth is dry. I can't reply to the text.

'Remember when you fell off that tree straight onto your back and you could not breathe for ages? You could have died then. That was pre-school.'

Yes I remember but my mind is totally numb by now. How to deal with this unexpected line of probing questions from cyberspace? Nothing like that has ever happened to me.

'So what?' I ask. It is the only thing I manage to utter. Was it too dismissive perhaps and lacking the awe and wonder one might have displayed by now? I feel so weird and disoriented, not knowing how to deal with this strange encounter.

'Remember that light reflecting shard on the hanger of Stoner Hill where Diane's ashes are interred? That was arranged to raise you up again.'

I nod without typing an answer.

'Remember that wandering light on the icon of Jesus Christ in your lounge above the mantelpiece? That too was done to help you up and reassure you that you are not alone, even if it often appears that way.'

I nod again feeling lightheaded and cornered at the same time.

'What is your name then?' I ask feebly.

'You can call me Toby'

'Toby who?'

'Toby or not to be, if you like. Excuse my sense of humour.
I am contacting you digitally, because you don't seem to
recognize the many signs that are coming your way. Perhaps I
can create some new spiritual awareness via this newfangled
iPhone technology.'

I am putting the iPhone away now. It is too much and outright
spooky. It is true, I am not easily convinced, not even by my

own hunches and I prefer to remain strictly rational at all times. It pings again.

'Remember all the good people I keep sending your way? There have been so many.'

'Where are you texting from Toby?'

'That would be telling, wouldn't it?'

'Why did you send untimely death and mental illness to my family? How could that ever have been helpful or protecting me in any way?

'You are not listening to me. I told you I was 'Personal Security'. We do not provide Family Cover. Everything is tailored individually.'

'Nobody is an island, Toby!'

'Don't wisecrack with me Heiner, we run the show. You are the pawns in our eternal game of chess. Coming and going. On the board one day, off the board next. And then on again for yet another round.'

'So why contact me, if I am nothing but a pawn on your game board?'

'You can be part of the game, make a difference, so that next time round you'll be more savvy. You may even become a Rook, a Bishop or a Knight. Eventually you can even become a Player.'

'I thought I was an autonomous player anyway. Free Will and all that? Have I got that wrong?'

'Well up to a point. Your hypothetical free will is dominated by biochemical algorithms and by your family values. Remember the Nature Nurture thing? They determine what you crave. I will guard you and help you if I think you deserve it, because your so-called autonomy and free will can easily land you in a Tsunami of all sorts of trouble. If I arrange a last minute day trip up to the snow covered mountains, you would be spared the ensuing floods miraculously without even realising that I had my hands on the wheel.'

'What is your advice then for my declining years right up to my last rites, just before you knock me off the chess board again? If I am still worthy of your attention at all, that is?'

'That was the point of my contacting you actually.'

'What do you mean Toby?'

'Whatever comes your way, be aware that you will always remain connected to a cosmic energy field and that you are part of God's creation. We know that you continue praying and searching for meaning. We don't expect membership of any self aggrandising faith corporation. They represent the needy perspectives of frail human psyches. We find them all charming and heartwarming. Whatever your creed Heiner, we will still consider you for another round of chess.'

I am choked by now and utterly bewildered, wanting to type some humble words of gratitude and appreciation to Toby. I open the IPhone again but somehow I can't find his entry anymore. Toby's numbers have disappeared entirely from my WhatsApp contact list. Have I inadvertently clicked a delete key? I check the Archive. Nothing. Have I merely imagined all of this? Toby's final message was so soothing and exactly what I needed to hear.

I check and check again. But there is nothing at all. Not now, anyway. Toby or not to be, indeed.

The Heavenly Chariot

We take it all for granted. It is almost impossible to be grateful for our blessings as almost none of us remember the days before electricity, before cars, before tap water. The scientific revolution has changed everything including our life expectancy, our forms of communication and our kind of entertainment.

Initially, science was based on simple observation, on experiment and on logical deduction, often supported by geometry and mathematics. It was a methodical way of gaining new knowledge by teasing out the secrets of nature that she had held so close to her chest from the beginning of time. Sapiens had finally reached a stage in his evolution where he could construct a wheel and work out the distance to the moon. His intrinsic curiosity had taken him away from being a cave dweller in East Africa so that he would eventually move into a skyscraper in New York.

But this universal nosiness of man has not always been welcomed by everybody. The Pharisees, the Popes and the

Mullahs objected to too much curiosity, as it seemed somewhat blasphemous to them. As far as the Religions of the Desert were concerned, all wisdom was contained in their holy books. They did not require a Library in Alexandria and one wonders why it finally went up in flames.

All those books and scrolls in Alexandria and elsewhere in the learned world were deemed to be not only superfluous but an offensive heresy because God himself knew all these things anyway. And if the Almighty had not imparted these secrets to us mortals directly, then there would have been a good reason for this. Our human tools of perception, they argued, were clearly limited out of divine precaution. Knowledge could be a dangerous thing if it fell into the wrong hands.

It may seem an imprudent thing to say these days, but is there not at least a kernel of truth in that old biblical sentiment? Today we have accumulated sufficient destructive potential to kill the global population many times over. Some would argue that we have eaten from the Tree of Knowledge against the decrees and wishes of the One who created us out of dust. Having been forced to live East of Eden, we have thrown away the shackles of religion almost entirely and can hardly recognise any sacredness anywhere at all.

One Christmas Eve many years ago, my good friend Bernard called around with an astonishing present, which he thought would suit my crazy predilection for sundialling and the history of astronomy. He told me that he had acquired an historic print in New York back in the 1950s. This very copy of the original print which was his Christmas present to me, turned out to be a copperplate engraving from 1680, created in Hamburg at a time in history when the problem of longitude calculation was far from being solved. That would take the best part of another hundred years until finally, in 1773, the carpenter and clockmaker John Harrison came up with a reliable maritime chronometer to work out longitude.

But the originators behind the design of this simple German engraving understood very well that at least in principle our round globe could be divided into 360° of longitude. Which specific longitude individual locations on this globe would be associated with, was still unknown, not least because nobody had yet agreed on a benchmark meridian against which all locations on this planet could be measured.

And therefore the authors of my old copperplate from 1680 had unilaterally declared Hamburg to be the zero meridian for the entire globe, at least for the time being and perhaps only for the purpose of this early planisphere. And as a result, all other locations around the entire world could be allocated their respective degrees of longitude, however imprecise the measurement of longitude might have been at the time. All this made fascinating reading and I spent hours poring over my maps, identifying the ancient names of the cities mentioned in this engraving. Where for example was Golconda? I had never heard of it in all my life.

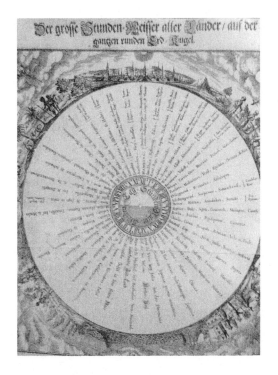

But the most amazing aspect of this planisphere was the curious inscription underneath the pictogram of our rotund home planet. Instead of celebrating the scientific achievement of this conceptual masterpiece, the text begins with a bitter complaint about the cheekiness and nosiness of these scientists, who wanted to know too much. Or were the publishers of this 'map' perhaps merely placating the Holy Roman Church by demonstrating that they were on the side of the Holy Book despite their pursuit of new knowledge?

143

The authors start their proud description of this showcase of contemporary understanding by humbling themselves and by questioning the wisdom of their very own undertaking. Was their global mapping project a symbol of disobedience and moral arrogance? Were the geographers from Hamburg perhaps fearing reprimand by the authorities for their forwardness in this whirlwind of a scientific revolution and discovery. Could such new knowledge in any way become dangerous and invalidate Scripture? The memory of the Church's treatment of Giordano Bruno and Galileo was still fresh in everybody's mind. The text thus begins with an amazing act of self flagellation and seems well worthy of our attention:

'Oh sacrilegious art, aping and copying all of nature's works of wonder. How dare she be so arrogant by planting a stake into the Earth wherever she pleases, surrounding it with numerals of all sorts, and then commanding the Sun to give account of his daily world-spanning journeys.'

'The Sun's heavenly chariot cannot progress one single step without his advances being registered by shadow marks which will be recognised and understood at once. This vertical stake is the day calendar, the indicator of the hour, witnessing all stages on its path and reducing its heavenly course artfully to our human scale.'

And then all modesty falls by the wayside and the technicalities of this illustrated planisphere can be proudly explained in full detail. I will only provide you with the flavour of the first paragraph of this account to show the departure from false contrition to justifiable scientific pride.

'The hour's gnomon, presented here, orders time in all the noblest countries and kingdoms, according to the Meridian here in Hamburg. When it is solar noon or midday here at home, the planisphere indicates which hour it be elsewhere around this globe by night or day. As for example, when it is midday here in Hamburg, so in Golconda it is the evening hour 6 o'clock or midnight in Berbudes or in San Jago morning 6 o'clock.'

How many scientists have published their results together with a critical assessment of their own work? It seems remarkable to see this juxtaposition of science and ethics or religion in one and the same publication. How often has this happened in the sciences? Should we see more of it? Or would that not be in line with the terms and conditions of modern R&D budget holders?

And so, despite the original objections and irritations of the religious nomenclature, scientific progress has become unstoppable and has led to a plethora of never ending discoveries and inventions. We can now not only draw a pictogram of our home planet but look back at our own Earth, rising above the horizon of a bleak Moonscape and furthermore we can see our terrestrial home as a mere speck of light from Mars. Where are we going next? And yet our own blue 'wanderer' is full of problems which almost appear to be beyond repair. As a species we do not seem particularly good at voluntary turning points.

145

Globalisation, overpopulation and perhaps even climate change would not have been possible without modern science. The positive outcomes of research often arrive with bad and unintended side effects.

Are we perhaps unintentionally contributing to our own demise while we are lost in thought, staring at our iPhones? To what extent have we passed the point of no return, the point after which there is no cure? Or can we solve all our current problems with ever more technology? Is there a technological fix after all or are we heading for some inevitable almighty crash, whether we want it or not. The author of 'Small is Beautiful' might have written a bestseller all those decades ago, but his message was certainly not heeded. Some fifty years ago Fritz Schumacher suggested, not without a hint of resignation:

> We have far too much knowledge
> to survive without wisdom.'

When the native American Indians encountered specimens of European invaders with their weird ideas of wanting to buy their Indian land, Chief Seattle, head of the Duwamish people is reported to have sent a letter to President Franklin Pierce in Washington, back in 1851. Two of the core paragraphs of his letter are of alarming topicality to this very day:

'The white man may discover one day that our God is the same God. You may think now that you own Him as you wish to own our land; but you cannot. He is the God of Man, and His compassion is equal for the red man and the white. This Earth is precious to Him, and to harm the Earth is to heap contempt on its Creator.'

'Your destiny is a mystery to us, for we do not understand what will be when the buffalo are all slaughtered, the wild horses are tamed, the secret corners of the forest heavy with the scent of many men, and the view of the ripe hills blotted by talking wires. Where will the thicket be? Gone! Where will the eagle be? Gone! And what is it to say goodbye to the swift pony and the hunt? It is the end of living and the beginning of survival.'

Perhaps the originators of my German copperplate pictogram were not too far out after all. Perhaps we should remain very cautious of the fruit we pick and eat from that famous Tree of Knowledge in the Garden of Eden.

Witch Hazel

Every January, in the midst of frost and winter,
When opening my bathroom window early
I gaze upon the wondrous Hazel Tree
Growing beyond the many roofs
There in my neighbour's garden.

Old neighbours leave and new ones come
The Hazel though has stayed and prospered
Grown into a sturdy tree
With solid arms stretching out wide.
Its twigs seem bare and frozen now.

Despite its wintry look
I know from all the years gone by
That there is life and sap and cryptic budding.
Thus kindling hope for longer days and brighter light.
The Hazel Tree will be the first to let me know.
And so I look for faintest hues of yellow
And swelling buds to thaw my inner frost.
One day, one day, all shall be fine for us
There will be love again and laughter,
Sweet music too and dance for all.

In early February it seemed as if it might be soon
That our Hazel Tree would smile again and open up.
A spell of cold began to test my patience though.
But by the 24th of Feb the Tree had kept its promise:
The rising sap had truly turned into a warming glow.

One day, one day, all shall be fine again
And love and laughter will be back
Sweet music too and dance for all.

Does this apply to aged folk like me?
With aching joints and music I can hardly hear?

For everything there is a season
A time for every purpose under Heaven.
A time for birth, a time to die.
What is my Hazel telling me this spring?
Which joys and earthly pleasures do remain?
Will there be trust that all is well?
I saw the Hazel Tree in bloom
when death knocked at my door.
It seemed so radiant when all of us
were scared of the pandemic.

And now with War in Eastern Europe
so very fast unfolding
The Hazel seems at its most radiant.

The Hazel and all other trees, don't seem to mind
who rules their land
Uncomprehending of human need for Kingdom
Willfully ignorant of human ambition,
of honour and of pride,
The Hazel shrugs at Presidents and Kings,
at Battle and at War
And at the blood somebody spilled
near that Town Hall today

And somewhere there,
amongst the smoking ruins of Mariupol
Amongst the shattered dreams of human kindness
and of generous compassion
There too, will shine a Hazel Tree in splendid bloom,
In frugal celebration of its roots and of its rising sap.
And all of us will stand in Shame and in Despair.

Mariupol March 2022

Printed in Great Britain
by Amazon

15664094R00088